INSPIRED CARDPLAY

David Bird is Britain's top bridge writer. Author of more than sixty bridge books, he is the creator of the famous 'Abbot' series. Martin Hoffman is known for his lightning-quick analysis and play of the cards. He plays professionally around the world and has a fine eye for unusual hands, those that require an unexpected move in the play.

In *Inspired Cardplay* Bird and Hoffman choose twelve critical areas of dummy play and defence. Each is illustrated by deals where the winning plays seem to be inspired. If truth be told, they are usually the result of careful observation and cold logic. With the authors' guidance you can train yourself to think along the right lines and greatly improve your own cardplay. If, instead you are perfectly happy with your own standard of performance, sit back in your chair and enjoy a thoroughly good read!

By DAVID BIRD *in the Master Bridge Series*

TEN WAYS TO IMPROVE YOUR BRIDGE
TOURNAMENT ACOL (with Tim Bourke)
ALL HANDS ON DECK!
BRIDGE OVER TROUBLED WATERS
FAMOUS BRIDGE DISASTERS
FAMOUS BRIDGE RECORDS (with Nikos Sarantakos)
BEATEN BY THE MASTERS

with Terence Reese
FAMOUS BIDDING DECISIONS
FAMOUS PLAY DECISIONS
FAMOUS LEADS AND DEFENCES

The Monastery Books
MIRACLES OF CARD PLAY
UNHOLY TRICKS: *More Miraculous Card Play*
DOUBLED AND VENERABLE: *Further Miracles of Card Play*
CARDINAL SINS
DIVINE INTERVENTION
THE ABBOT AND THE SENSATIONAL SQUEEZE

with Ron Klinger
KOSHER BRIDGE
KOSHER BRIDGE 2
THE RABBI'S MAGIC TRICK: *More Kosher Bridge*

with Simon Cochemé
BACHELOR BRIDGE: *the Amorous Adventures of Jack O'Hearts*
BRIDGE WITH A FEMININE TOUCH

INSPIRED
CARDPLAY

David Bird &
Martin Hoffman

CASSELL
IN ASSOCIATION WITH
PETER CRAWLEY

First published in Great Britain 2003
in association with Peter Crawley
by Cassell
Wellington House,
125 Strand, London WC2R 0BB
an imprint of the Orion Publishing Group Ltd

ISBN 0-304-36586-6

Printed and Bound in Great Britain by
Clays Ltd, St. Ives plc

CONTENTS

1
Combining Options

There is usually more than one chance of making a contract. Whenever possible, you should aim to combine two or more chances instead of relying on the best single chance.

We will start with a straightforward example, a deal that was misplayed at the St James's Club in London.

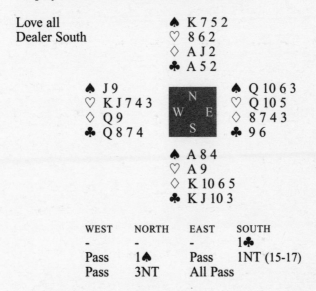

Love all
Dealer South

♠ K 7 5 2
♡ 8 6 2
◇ A J 2
♣ A 5 2

♠ J 9
♡ K J 7 4 3
◇ Q 9
♣ Q 8 7 4

♠ Q 10 6 3
♡ Q 10 5
◇ 8 7 4 3
♣ 9 6

♠ A 8 4
♡ A 9
◇ K 10 6 5
♣ K J 10 3

WEST	NORTH	EAST	SOUTH
-	-	-	1♣
Pass	1♠	Pass	1NT (15-17)
Pass	3NT	All Pass	

West led the ♡4 to East's queen. Declarer ducked the first heart and won the ♡10 continuation with the ace, noting West's ♡3. Hearts were clearly 5-3 and nine tricks would have to be scored without surrendering the lead.

The original declarer viewed the situation merely as 'which minor-suit finesse should I take?' A successful club finesse through East would land the contract however the suit broke, which was not true of a successful diamond finesse. Also, the 5-3

heart break rather suggested that East was a favourite to hold the
♣Q. Declarer crossed to the ace of clubs and finessed the club
jack, bemoaning his luck when this lost and the game went down.

What did you make of that? There was no need to bank
everything on one chance. When you are missing two queens, you
should play for the drop in one suit before taking a finesse in the
other. Generally you play for the drop in the suit where you have
the longer combined holding, because that queen is more likely to
fall. Here the lengths in the minors are the same. Can you see why
it is better to play for the drop in one suit rather than the other?

You should play for the drop in diamonds. If the ◊Q does not
drop, your residual chance will
then be a full 50%. If instead
you try to drop the ♣Q and
fail, your residual chance in
diamonds will be less than
50%. Here virtue is rewarded.
The ◊Q falls and you make
the game.

> **TOP TIP**
>
> When faced with an apparent choice
> of queen finesses, combine playing
> for the drop in one suit with a finesse
> in the other. Play for the drop in the
> suit where you hold more cards.

The next deal arose in a Far East Championship. At least one
declarer failed in a grand slam that should have been made.

Game all
Dealer South

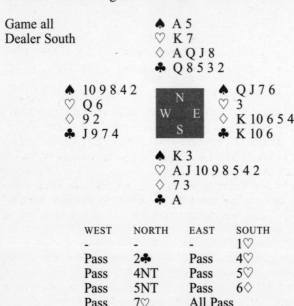

        ♠ A 5
        ♡ K 7
        ◊ A Q J 8
        ♣ Q 8 5 3 2

♠ 10 9 8 4 2   ♠ Q J 7 6
♡ Q 6   ♡ 3
◊ 9 2   ◊ K 10 6 5 4
♣ J 9 7 4   ♣ K 10 6

        ♠ K 3
        ♡ A J 10 9 8 5 4 2
        ◊ 7 3
        ♣ A

WEST	NORTH	EAST	SOUTH
-	-	-	1♡
Pass	2♣	Pass	4♡
Pass	4NT	Pass	5♡
Pass	5NT	Pass	6◊
Pass	7♡	All Pass	

South's 6◇ indicated one side-suit king. Hoping that this would be helpfully placed in one of the minors, North potted the grand slam. How would you play this contract when the ♠10 is led?

It's hard to believe, in an international championship, but at least one declarer simply drew trumps and took the diamond finesse. The diamond king was unsympathetically placed and a minus score ensued. A better idea is to take two club ruffs before relying on the diamond finesse. If the ♣K happens to fall in three rounds you can discard a diamond.

How should the play go? You win the spade lead in your hand, cash the ♣A and cross to the king of trumps. After taking one club ruff, you draw the outstanding trump, return to dummy with the spade ace and ruff another club. The king appears from East and you can reach dummy's established queen of clubs with a diamond to the ace. No excuse at all for going down on that one!

On the same deal a Japanese declarer in the youth championship reached the grand slam in hearts and received the apparently lethal lead of the ◇9, removing an entry to dummy. Unwilling to believe that West had led from the diamond king, he rose with the ace of diamonds. He then

> ### TOP TIP
>
> Many players miss the extra-chance play of ruffing out a defender's honour. When dummy has Q-x-x-x opposite a singleton ace, or J-x-x-x opposite A-K bare, there is a worthwhile chance that you can ruff out the missing key honour.

crossed to the ace of clubs and led a low trump finessing dummy's seven! When this entry-creating manoeuvre succeeded he was back on track for the secondary chance in clubs. He ruffed a club, returned to dummy with the king of trumps and ruffed another club. The youngster's bravery was rewarded when the ♣K fell to the baize. The spade ace remained as an entry to dummy's club winners.

On the next deal declarer could see more than one chance of making his contract. Unfortunately he failed to spot yet another chance, the one that would have succeeded.

Game all　　　　♠ 7 6 4
Dealer South　　♡ K J 9 7 5
　　　　　　　　♢ 8 5 4
　　　　　　　　♣ A 4

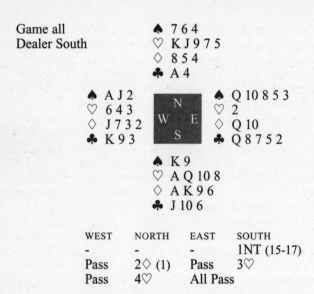

```
            ♠ A J 2              ♠ Q 10 8 5 3
            ♡ 6 4 3       N      ♡ 2
            ♢ J 7 3 2   W   E    ♢ Q 10
            ♣ K 9 3       S      ♣ Q 8 7 5 2
                       ♠ K 9
                       ♡ A Q 10 8
                       ♢ A K 9 6
                       ♣ J 10 6
```

WEST	NORTH	EAST	SOUTH
-	-	-	1NT (15-17)
Pass	2♢ (1)	Pass	3♡
Pass	4♡	All Pass	

(1) Transfer response, showing at least five hearts.

South broke the transfer and arrived in four hearts. He won the trump lead and drew trumps in two more rounds. There were two obvious chances of making the game. If diamonds were 3-3 he could discard a club from dummy on the long diamond. Failing that, he would need to find the ♠A onside.

Declarer cashed the ace of diamonds, the ten falling on his right. It was only at this moment that a small problem concerning entries became apparent. If he continued with king and another diamond, setting up a third winner in the suit, he would have no convenient entry to his hand to enjoy the long diamond. He could not use a fourth round of trumps for this purpose because his last trump was needed to ruff dummy's last spade.

Deciding that he would have to retain the ♢K as an entry to his hand, declarer led a low diamond on the second round. Unfortunately for him, this gave up on the chance of East holding Q-10 or J-10 doubleton. East won the second round of diamonds with the queen and switched to a spade, the defenders taking two tricks in the suit. When the diamond suit failed to break 3-3, declarer had to lose a club and went one down.

Do you see where declarer made his mistake? It was when he drew the third round of trumps... in other words, a second or two before he paused to plan the play! If he draws only two rounds of trumps and then plays, ace, king and another diamond he will still make the contract when diamonds are 3-3. He can re-enter his hand with the third round of trumps. By playing the hand in this fashion, he adds a third option to his list — that two honours will fall doubleton from the defender who does not hold the last trump. Not a huge extra edge, we concede, but it was worth 12 IMPs on this occasion.

> **TOP TIP**
>
> Before drawing trumps, check that you will not need later the entries that the trump suit provides. An obvious situation where you should delay drawing trumps is when you plan to ruff good a suit in dummy and will need dummy's third and final trump as an entry.

Our next example of combining options was played by Al Kahn, in a match at the Sunrise Lakes Club in Florida.

East-West game
Dealer South

```
                    ♠ K 7 2
                    ♡ A 3
                    ♢ K 9 8 6 5
                    ♣ A 7 2
   ♠ Q 10 5                        ♠ J 9 4
   ♡ J 9 8 6 5 2    N              ♡ Q 10 4
   ♢ 2            W   E            ♢ Q J 10 7
   ♣ 9 4 3          S              ♣ K J 5
                    ♠ A 8 6 3
                    ♡ K 7
                    ♢ A 4 3
                    ♣ Q 10 8 6
```

WEST	NORTH	EAST	SOUTH
-	-	-	1♣
Pass	1♢	Pass	1NT (12-14)
Pass	3NT	All Pass	

At both tables the ♡6 was led to the queen and king. The declarer at the other table was soon down. He ducked a diamond at Trick 2, won the heart continuation and had no chance when diamonds proved to be 4-1. Kahn followed a stronger line. At Trick 2 he cashed the ♢A. This directly improved his chances of scoring four diamond tricks, since if East had started with a singleton queen, jack or ten a subsequent finesse of dummy's $\diamond$9 would land the contract.

Only small cards appeared under the diamond ace and Kahn continued with another diamond, West showing out. Do you see how much better placed he was than his counterpart at the other table? Aware of the bad diamond break in good time, he could rise with the $\diamond$K and play for the clubs to be well disposed. The best play for three club tricks is to cash the ace and then play to the ten. No guess was required, in practice, since East turned up

> **TOP TIP**
>
> By cashing the top honours, instead of ducking the first round, you can discover whether a suit breaks without losing the lead. This may enable you to play for a different chance in good time.

with a helpful ♣K-J-x. Declarer scored three club tricks and two further tricks in each of the other suits.

When the second-best chance in a suit will leave you with another chance elsewhere, it may be the one to take. Look at this deal:

North-South game
Dealer South

```
                    ♠ A Q J
                    ♡ 10 5
                    ◇ J 9 8 7 3
                    ♣ 6 5 3
  ♠ 9 6 5 2                        ♠ 8 7 4
  ♡ Q 7          N                 ♡ 8 6 3
  ◇ 6 2       W     E              ◇ Q 10 5 4
  ♣ 10 9 8 7 4      S              ♣ K Q 2
                    ♠ K 10 3
                    ♡ A K J 9 4 2
                    ◇ A K
                    ♣ A J
```

WEST	NORTH	EAST	SOUTH
-	-	-	2♣
Pass	2◇	Pass	2♡
Pass	3◇	Pass	3♡
Pass	6♡	All Pass	

What is your plan when ♣10 is led to East's queen?

You could cross to dummy with a spade and bank everything on the best play in the trump suit (a finesse). If it failed, you would be dead — the defenders would cash a club trick. A better idea is to combine the second-best play in trumps (playing for the drop) with the chance of setting up a diamond to discard your club loser.

After winning the club lead, you should cash the ace and king of trumps. When the trump queen falls, your problems are over. Suppose instead that trumps break 3-2 but the queen does not fall. You then play the two top diamonds. If the other red queen falls, you will cross to dummy and take a club discard on the diamond jack. Otherwise you will cross to the ♠Q and ruff a diamond. When diamonds are 3-3 you will again be able to throw your club loser. Sometimes you will make the contract even when a defender holds four diamonds to the queen. Suppose East's shape is 3-3-4-3, as in the diagram, but his trumps are Q-6-3. You will be able to set up the thirteenth diamond and take your discard at Trick 11. Combining two chances in this way gives you a much better total chance than relying only on the best play in the trump suit (finessing against the queen).

TOP TIP

Missing five trumps to the queen, the best single-suit play is to finesse. Playing for the drop instead can be beneficial when it allows you to pursue a second chance without losing the lead.

On the next deal there are at least three possible lines of play. Your choice will depend on the lie of the trumps.

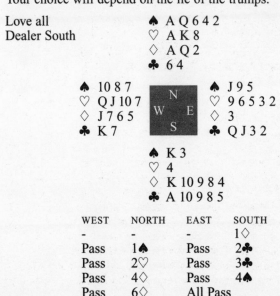

Love all
Dealer South

♠ A Q 6 4 2
♡ A K 8
◇ A Q 2
♣ 6 4

♠ 10 8 7
♡ Q J 10 7
◇ J 7 6 5
♣ K 7

♠ J 9 5
♡ 9 6 5 3 2
◇ 3
♣ Q J 3 2

♠ K 3
♡ 4
◇ K 10 9 8 4
♣ A 10 9 8 5

WEST	NORTH	EAST	SOUTH
-	-	-	1◇
Pass	1♠	Pass	2♣
Pass	2♡	Pass	3♣
Pass	4◇	Pass	4♠
Pass	6◇	All Pass	

West leads the ♡Q, removing a potentially useful entry to dummy. How will you continue?

The original declarer thought he had made a good effort. He won the heart lead, played a spade to the king and returned to dummy with a trump. After discarding a spade on the ♡K, he ruffed a spade in his hand, protecting himself against a 4-2 spade break. When he crossed back to dummy with a trump, East showed out and the contract was in tatters.

The best move at Trick 2 is a low trump, away from the ace-queen. If the ◇J happens to fall singleton, you can adopt Plan 1: play ace and another club and plan to take a club ruff with one of dummy's honours. When the trump jack does not appear, cash the ♠K and return to dummy with the trump ace. Should trumps break 3-2, follow Plan 2: the original declarer's line of throwing a spade and ruffing a spade, to cater for a 4-2 spade break. When trumps divide 4-1, Plan 3 is to hope that the spades break 3-3. If they do, you can throw all four club losers from the South hand. West can ruff whenever he chooses. You will be able to win his return and cross to the ◇Q, drawing his last trump.

Here is one more example of combining the chances in trumps and a side suit. Try it for yourself.

North-South game
Dealer North

	♠ Q 5 2	
	♡ A Q 10 5 2	
	◇ A J	
	♣ 7 4 2	

♠ J 7 4		♠ K 3
♡ J 7 6	N	♡ K 9 8 4
◇ 7 5 4	W E	◇ Q 10 9 8 3 2
♣ J 9 8 6	S	♣ 10

	♠ A 10 9 8 6	
	♡ 3	
	◇ K 6	
	♣ A K Q 5 3	

WEST	NORTH	EAST	SOUTH
-	1♡	Pass	1♠
Pass	2♠	Pass	3♣
Pass	3♠	Pass	4NT
Pass	5♡	Pass	6♠
All Pass			

The bidding was questionable, since with only three-card spade support, North should have bid 3♡ or 3NT at his third turn. Even so, there was nothing wrong with the final contract. How would you play the spade slam after a diamond lead?

The original declarer won the diamond lead in his hand and continued with the ace of trumps followed by the ten, a low card appearing from West. After an agonised trance he ran the ten, brightening when it forced East's king. He won the diamond return and now had to draw the last trump. (There was no question of playing on clubs, possibly ruffing the fourth round, because ruffing with dummy's queen would set up the defenders' jack). The club suit broke 4-1 and the slam went one down.

Even looking at the trump suit in isolation, declarer did not take the percentage play. It is better to lead the suit twice from dummy, taking two finesses. This picks up the suit for one loser when East holds either honour. You should win the diamond lead in dummy and play a trump to the ten and jack. After winning the diamond continuation in your hand, cross to the ace of hearts and lead the queen of trumps (in case East has K-x-x remaining). As it happens, the king appears and you win with the ace.

Before drawing the last trump you test the clubs by playing the ace and king. If the suit breaks 3-2, draw the last trump and claim. If clubs are 4-1 you can still make the contract when the last trump lies with the club length, as in the diagram. You cash the club queen, ruff a club and return to hand with a heart ruff to draw the last trump. This extra chance play would still be available when East started with K-x-x in the trump suit. Only when East began with K-x-x-x would you have to draw trumps and rely on a favourable club division.

> **TOP TIP**
>
> Suppose you are playing in a 5-3 trump fit with a side-suit such as x-x-x in dummy and A-K-Q-x(-x) in your hand. You can give yourself an extra chance by drawing only two rounds of trumps before testing the side suit. When the defender with four cards in the side suit also holds the last trump, you can take a ruff in dummy. If the other defender ruffs, you have lost nothing.

On the next deal declarer failed to combine two options for the good reason that he could see only one option. How good would your eyesight have been?

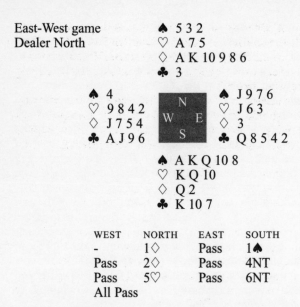

East-West game
Dealer North

♠ 5 3 2
♡ A 7 5
◇ A K 10 9 8 6
♣ 3

♠ 4
♡ 9 8 4 2
◇ J 7 5 4
♣ A J 9 6

♠ J 9 7 6
♡ J 6 3
◇ 3
♣ Q 8 5 4 2

♠ A K Q 10 8
♡ K Q 10
◇ Q 2
♣ K 10 7

WEST	NORTH	EAST	SOUTH
-	1◇	Pass	1♠
Pass	2◇	Pass	4NT
Pass	5♡	Pass	6NT
All Pass			

West led the ♡8, won in the South hand, and declarer began by cashing the ace and king of spades. West showed out on the second round and declarer crossed to dummy with the ♡A to take the marked finesse of the ♠10. He could then count eleven tricks on top — thirteen, with tricks to spare, if the diamond suit came in.

Declarer played the last two spade winners, throwing a club and a diamond from dummy. These cards remained:

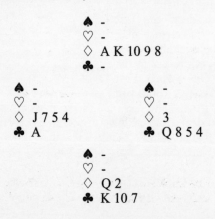

♠ -
♡ -
◇ A K 10 9 8
♣ -

♠ -
♡ -
◇ J 7 5 4
♣ A

♠ -
♡ -
◇ 3
♣ Q 8 5 4

♠ -
♡ -
◇ Q 2
♣ K 10 7

Declarer cashed the queen of diamonds and played a diamond to the ace. If the suit had broken 3-2 he could have claimed an overtrick. As the cards lay, everything went sour. Declarer had to concede two tricks to West and the slam went one down. Do you see where he went wrong?

As declarer needed only four diamond tricks for the contract, not five, he should have discarded another diamond from dummy, retaining a low club. When two rounds of diamonds exposed the break in that suit, these cards would be left:

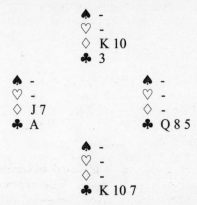

A club to the seven and ace forces West to give two tricks to the dummy.

You will succeed also against a different lie of the club suit:

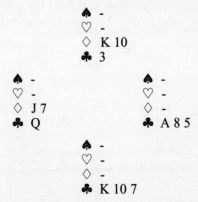

Again you lead the ♣3 to your seven. Either West is end-played or East rises with the ace and has to give you two club tricks.

2
Entry Planning

Managing your entries is one of the most important aspects of cardplay. In this chapter we will study some deals where entries to one hand or other are sparse and special steps have to be taken.

On the first deal you must plan the entire play before deciding where to win the first trick.

Love all
Dealer South

	♠ A 9 8 7 5 4	
	♡ 8 6 3	
	◇ K 7 2	
	♣ 2	

♠ Q J 6		♠ 10 3
♡ K J 10	N	♡ Q 5 4 2
◇ 10 9 3	W E	◇ J 8 5 4
♣ A J 10 7	S	♣ K 6 3

	♠ K 2	
	♡ A 9 7	
	◇ A Q 6	
	♣ Q 9 8 5 4	

WEST	NORTH	EAST	SOUTH
-	-	-	1NT (15-17)
Pass	2♡	Pass	2♠
Pass	4♠	All Pass	

North makes a transfer response and then overbids somewhat, promoting you to a dubious spade game. Do you see any chance when West leads the ◇10?

The defenders are threatening to score one trump, two hearts and a club. To stand any chance you must establish a long club.

Since this will require several entries to the South hand, it is clear to win the diamond lead with dummy's king. After a club to the nine and ten, West switches to a heart. You win with the ace and ruff a club. All follow to the ace and king of trumps and — edging towards your goal — you take another club ruff. A diamond to the ace allows you to lead a fourth round of clubs. West produces the last club, you ruff in dummy and – yes! – East cannot overruff.

A third round of diamonds to the queen stands up, leaving you in the South hand. These cards remain:

The hard work done, you lead the established queen of clubs. West has to ruff to prevent this card becoming your tenth trick and dummy's ♠9 is promoted. Game made!

On the next deal, the only threat to the contract is obvious — a bad trump break. You must plan how to deal with this potential problem right at the start, not when the hand has started to fall apart and it is too late to recover.

TOP TIP

Suppose you are in a major-suit game with a trump holding of A-x-x-x-x-x opposite K-x and three unavoidable side-suit losers. It may seem hopeless but if you are able to score all the trumps in the long hand, by taking several ruffs, you can sometimes condense four losers into three. The defender with the master trump will have to ruff one of his partner's winners at the end.

East-West game
Dealer South

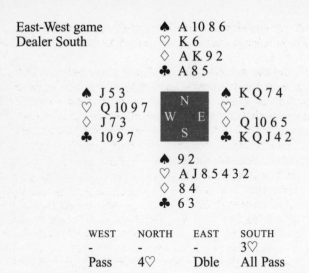

♠ A 10 8 6
♡ K 6
◇ A K 9 2
♣ A 8 5

♠ J 5 3
♡ Q 10 9 7
◇ J 7 3
♣ 10 9 7

♠ K Q 7 4
♡ -
◇ Q 10 6 5
♣ K Q J 4 2

♠ 9 2
♡ A J 8 5 4 3 2
◇ 8 4
♣ 6 3

WEST	NORTH	EAST	SOUTH
-	-	-	3♡
Pass	4♡	Dble	All Pass

West leads the ♣10 against your doubled game in hearts. The bidding suggests that West may hold four trumps. Even if it did not, you would base your play on that assumption because it is the only serious risk to your contract. You have two clear-cut losers in the black suits. If trumps do break 4-0 how can you avoid two further losers in the trump suit?

The general plan will be to take as many ruffs as possible with the low trumps in the South hand. Near the end of the play you hope to throw West on lead, forcing him to lead a trump into your A-J tenace.

> **TOP TIP**
>
> When a bad trump break is the only serious risk to your contract, plan the play on the assumption that the trumps do indeed break as badly as you fear.

To prepare for the black-suit ruffs, you need to duck a round of each suit. So, duck the ♣10 lead and win the club continuation with the ace. You can then afford to cash the king of hearts to check the trump situation. They are 4-0, as you suspected, and East discards a club. What now?

If you mistakenly ruff a club before ducking a spade, a fourth round of clubs from East will allow West to overruff you. He will then exit safely and await the setting trick in trumps. Only one play is good enough at this stage — you must duck a round of spades, leaving the spade ace in dummy. Let's say that East wins the first round of spades and continues with another club. You ruff in the South hand, cross to the ace of spades and ruff a spade.

After cashing the ace-king of diamonds, you must take one more ruff in your hand. To avoid an overruff, you will need to identify West's last plain card. East's take-out double of 4♡ strongly suggests that the spades started 3-4. If East (who has thrown one club and followed to three rounds) has retained an honour as his last card, you will also have a count on the club suit. Perhaps the defenders gave you a count when you played on diamonds. In any of these situations you will know, on the present deal, that West has a diamond remaining. Even if the defend-

> **TOP TIP**
>
> Defenders who use count signals usually signal honestly. They benefit considerably from the information exchanged As declarer, you must offset this by taking advantage of the signals yourself.

ers gave nothing away, the a priori likelihood with seven diamonds and eight clubs missing, is that West started 3-3 in these suits.

You ruff a diamond in your hand, pleased to see West follow suit. These cards remain:

The hard labour is over — only the pleasure remains. You lead ♡8 from your hand and face your remaining two cards.

Entries were a problem on the next hand, too, where a young declarer at the Maccabiah Games in Tel Aviv played too quickly.

North-South game
Dealer South

♠ K Q
♡ K
♢ A K J 10 3 2
♣ K Q J 9

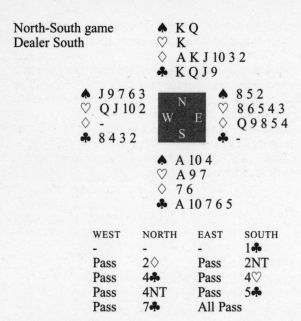

♠ J 9 7 6 3
♡ Q J 10 2
♢ -
♣ 8 4 3 2

♠ 8 5 2
♡ 8 6 5 4 3
♢ Q 9 8 5 4
♣ -

♠ A 10 4
♡ A 9 7
♢ 7 6
♣ A 10 7 6 5

WEST	NORTH	EAST	SOUTH
-	-	-	1♣
Pass	2♢	Pass	2NT
Pass	4♣	Pass	4♡
Pass	4NT	Pass	5♣
Pass	7♣	All Pass	

West led the ♡Q against the grand slam in clubs and declarer was well pleased with the dummy. He won with dummy's king and was about to claim the contract when East showed out on the first round of trumps. There were still thirteen tricks available, in a way, but communications were a problem. Declarer reasoned that since East was short in clubs he was likely to be long in diamonds. In that case the suit could surely be set up with a ruffing finesse.

Declarer drew all the trumps and then played a diamond towards the dummy. When West showed out, declarer's plan collapsed. He could set up just one extra trick in diamonds and entry problems would stop him from scoring the third diamond trick as well as all his winners in the majors. If he left a top spade in dummy, to reach the third diamond trick, he would have to abandon the spade ace. Do you see where declarer went wrong?

If declarer scores a heart ruff in dummy, he can afford to abandon one of his winners. When trumps prove to be 4-0, he should make the key play of overtaking the king of spades with the ace. He can then ruff a heart and play dummy's two remaining trumps, overtaking in the South hand to draw the last trump. One of dummy's low diamonds goes on the fourth trump, the other is thrown on the ace of hearts. It is then a simple matter to cash the two top diamonds, take the ruffing finesse in diamonds and return to dummy with the ♠Q to enjoy the established diamond. Count the tricks that are made: two spades, two hearts, three diamonds, five trumps and... a heart ruff in dummy. Had dummy's spade queen been a low spot-card instead, the successful line would have been easier to see!

The next deal comes from a teams-of-four match. The winning play is simple, once you spot it, but it would be beyond many players. Be brave and put yourself to the test (no-one's watching). Would you have made the contract?

Love all   ♠ 2
Dealer North   ♡ A K Q 9 7
       ◇ 8 6 4 3
       ♣ A 6 2

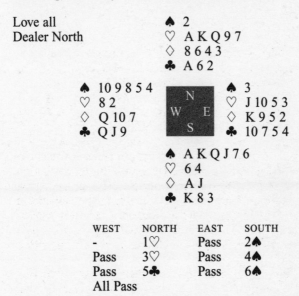

 ♠ 10 9 8 5 4   ♠ 3
 ♡ 8 2   ♡ J 10 5 3
 ◇ Q 10 7   ◇ K 9 5 2
 ♣ Q J 9   ♣ 10 7 5 4

     ♠ A K Q J 7 6
     ♡ 6 4
     ◇ A J
     ♣ K 8 3

WEST	NORTH	EAST	SOUTH
-	1♡	Pass	2♠
Pass	3♡	Pass	4♠
Pass	5♣	Pass	6♠
All Pass			

A diamond lead would have worked well but West led the ♣Q. How would you play the slam when two rounds of trumps reveal the 5-1 break?

The original declarer won the club lead in his hand. Worried that the apparently excellent grand slam would be bid at the other table, he played two rounds of trumps. The 5-1 trump break was good news in a way, since the grand would now fail. Twelve tricks still had to be made, however. He cashed two of dummy's top hearts, leaving these cards out:

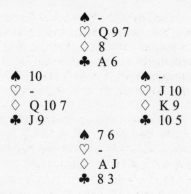

'Queen of hearts, please,' said the declarer, throwing a club.

West ruffed the heart queen and the slam could no longer be made. Do you see where declarer went wrong?

It was as late as in the six-card end position shown above. Instead of trying to cash the ♡Q declarer should ruff a low heart in the South hand. There is nothing West can do. If he overruffs, dummy's remaining hearts will provide discards for declarer's two minor-suit losers. If West refuses to overruff, declarer will concede a trick to West's master trump. Again twelve tricks will be there.

Have you ever overcalled an opponent's 2NT opening? South achieved the feat on the next deal, albeit in the protective position.

East-West game
Dealer West

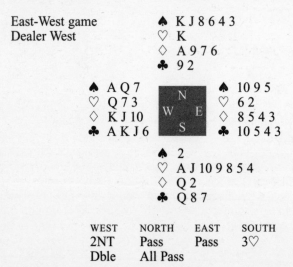

♠ K J 8 6 4 3
♡ K
◇ A 9 7 6
♣ 9 2

♠ A Q 7
♡ Q 7 3
◇ K J 10
♣ A K J 6

♠ 10 9 5
♡ 6 2
◇ 8 5 4 3
♣ 10 5 4 3

♠ 2
♡ A J 10 9 8 5 4
◇ Q 2
♣ Q 8 7

WEST	NORTH	EAST	SOUTH
2NT	Pass	Pass	3♡
Dble	All Pass		

South, who could tell from the opponents' limited auction that his partner would hold some points, ventured a 3♡ overcall. West doubled, as players do, although for a 2NT opening his hand was not particularly strong in defence. He led a top club, receiving a discouraging signal from his partner, and switched to a trump. Take the South cards now. How will you play the contract?

The deal comes from a teams-of-four match with both declarers in the same contract. The first declarer won the trump switch with dummy's king and exited with the king of spades. West was end-played in four suits and had to concede some ground. He chose to exit with the king of diamonds. Although declarer now had two diamond tricks, he was still left with five losers: one spade, one trump and three clubs.

At the other table declarer overtook dummy's king of trumps with the ace at Trick 2! This cost him nothing since it was clear from West's double that the trump queen would not be doubleton. Taking advantage of the extra entry to his hand, he led a spade towards dummy. West rose with the ace and exited safely with queen and another trump. However, when the trumps were run he was hopelessly squeezed in three suits. This was the end position:

> **TOP TIP**
>
> There are many situations where it pays you to overtake a bare honour with a higher honour in the hand where you hold length. Suppose you hold a bare Q opposite K-10-9-8-7-4. Overtake the queen with the king and two side entries to the hand with the long suit will suffice to bring in the suit and enjoy it. Fail to overtake and the defenders may hold up the ace. You will then need three entries.

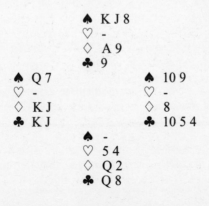

West threw the ♣J on the next trump. To avoid any guesswork (West might have had two clubs left, alongside a bare ◇K), declarer continued with his last trump, forcing West to throw the ◇J. At this stage either the ◇K or the ♠Q was known to be bare in the West hand. Declarer crossed to the ace of diamonds and the diamond king fell. Had it not fallen, the spade queen would have fallen instead.

We will end the chapter with a couple of deals where the defenders have to work cleverly to develop an entry. The first one arose in the teams final of an Israeli Bridge Festival. The match, between French and Israeli teams, had been hard-fought and all depended on the very last deal:

Love all
Dealer North

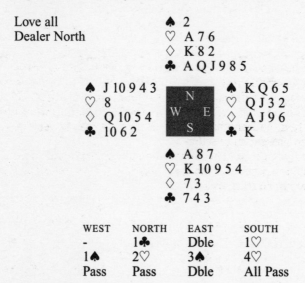

	♠	2
	♡	A 7 6
	◇	K 8 2
	♣	A Q J 9 8 5

♠ J 10 9 4 3		♠ K Q 6 5
♡ 8		♡ Q J 3 2
◇ Q 10 5 4		◇ A J 9 6
♣ 10 6 2		♣ K

	♠	A 8 7
	♡	K 10 9 5 4
	◇	7 3
	♣	7 4 3

WEST	NORTH	EAST	SOUTH
-	1♣	Dble	1♡
1♠	2♡	3♠	4♡
Pass	Pass	Dble	All Pass

The French East knew that his partner would be short in hearts and might have taken the winning decision to bid game in spades. No, he preferred to double 4♡. Shaya Levit, the declarer, won the ♠J lead with the ace and ruffed a spade. Realising that he would not have the entries to pick up ♣K-x-x with West, Levit's next move was to cash dummy's ace of clubs. Good news arrived in the shape of East's king. Aiming to shorten East's trumps, declarer called for the queen of clubs. When East ruffed and returned the ♠K, Levit could see that the entry situation would be hopeless if he ruffed with dummy's ♡7. He ruffed instead with the ace, leaving this position:

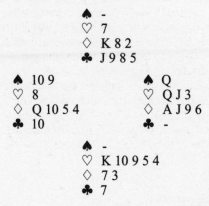

Take the East cards now. What will you do when declarer calls for dummy's last trump?

The French East defended weakly, following with the ♡3. Levit finessed the ten successfully. When East was thrown on lead with king and another trump, he had to take his ace of diamonds to prevent an overtrick.

East does better to split his trump honours. Declarer wins with the king and returns the ten of trumps to East's remaining honour, leaving these cards still out:

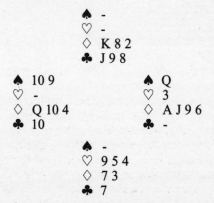

Now comes the clever bit. East cannot return the ♠Q because declarer will simply ruff and draw the last trump. Instead East must play the jack of diamonds! Declarer has to win with dummy's king but he has no entry to his hand, to draw the last trump. When he tries a low diamond from dummy, East allows his partner to win with the queen and receives a well deserved club ruff. It's a pity that East never gave himself the chance to find such a pretty defence. Had he done so, his efforts might have been written up in some book or other.

Our other defensive deal bears some similarity to the first. Once again the spotlight swings towards East.

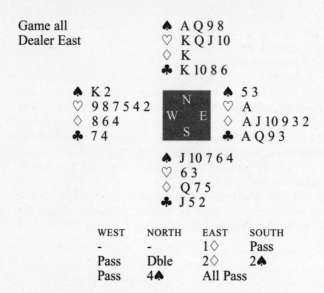

Game all	♠ A Q 9 8
Dealer East	♡ K Q J 10
	◇ K
	♣ K 10 8 6

	♠ K 2		♠ 5 3
	♡ 9 8 7 5 4 2	N	♡ A
	◇ 8 6 4	W E	◇ A J 10 9 3 2
	♣ 7 4	S	♣ A Q 9 3

	♠ J 10 7 6 4
	♡ 6 3
	◇ Q 7 5
	♣ J 5 2

WEST	NORTH	EAST	SOUTH
-	-	1◇	Pass
Pass	Dble	2◇	2♠
Pass	4♠	All Pass	

If East had rebid 2♣ instead of 2◇, he might have attracted a club lead, which would put the spade game a massive four down. (The defenders score two ruffs and the fourth round of clubs then promotes West's ♠K.) As it was, West led the ◇6, second-best from a bad suit, East winning dummy's bare king with the ace. Suppose you had been East after this start. How would you plot declarer's downfall?

The original East player deduced that prospects for the defence were very poor unless West held the king of trumps. He cashed the bare ♡A and continued with the ◇J, hoping that declarer would have to ruff in the dummy and would not then be able to reach his hand to take a trump finesse.

The plan failed to materialise. Declarer produced the diamond queen at Trick 3 and picked up the trumps with a finesse. He then discarded two clubs on dummy's heart suit, making the game exactly.

It was unlikely that West held the ♠K and the ◇Q. East should instead have attempted to reach his partner's hand in the club suit, in order to receive a heart ruff. This can be done if West holds three clubs to the jack or any doubleton club. After cashing the ace of hearts, East should switch to the ♣Q – a similar play to that on the previous

> **TOP TIP**
>
> When, in defence, you hold A-Q-x or A-J-x over a guarded king in dummy, you may be able to reach your partner's hand by leading the queen or jack. If declarer wins with the king, you will lead a low card to partner's hoped-for honour later. If instead declarer allows your honour to win, you will score two tricks in the suit anyway.

deal. West will signal with the ♣7 and dummy's king will win. Declarer will go down for sure if he plays on either major suit at this stage. If he is suspicious that East's ♡A was a singleton, his only other option is to lead a club from dummy.

East will then be faced with a critical decision. If West started with J-x-x in the club suit he must play low, allowing West to win with the jack and deliver a heart ruff. If instead West started with a doubleton club, East must instead rise with the club ace and give partner a club ruff. Which play should he attempt here, do you think?

Count signals would give East the answer. On the present deal West's high spot-card signal (the seven) on the first round of clubs suggests that he has a doubleton. East should rise with the ace and two ruffs will follow for two down. Had West started with J-x-x in the club suit he would have shown count with his lowest spot-card. East would then duck the second round of clubs – taking his only chance, that West holds the jack.

> **TOP TIP**
>
> Count signals (high to show an even number of cards, low to show an odd number) resolve countless problems in defence. If you have never tried them, you will be amazed how well they work. At Trick 1 you can get the best of both worlds by leading an ace or queen to request an attitude signal, a king to request a count signal. In other words, you vary your lead from A-K and K-Q according to the signal you require.

3
Elimination Play

The most familiar type of elimination play is the 'ruff-and-discard elimination'. The defender who is thrown on lead has the choice between playing on a suit, to your advantage, or giving you a ruff-and-discard. We will open the chapter with some slightly unusual examples of this form of play.

East-West game
Dealer South

	♠ Q 8 5
	♡ A K 6 3
	◇ 8 7 5 2
	♣ K 6

♠ K 7 4 2		♠ 9 6 3
♡ 8		♡ 9 5 4
◇ Q 10 4	W E	◇ J 6
♣ J 10 9 7 4		♣ Q 8 5 3 2

	♠ A J 10
	♡ Q J 10 7 2
	◇ A K 9 3
	♣ A

WEST	NORTH	EAST	SOUTH
-	-	-	1♡
Pass	3NT	Pass	4NT
Pass	5♡	Pass	6♡
All Pass			

North's 3NT showed a sound raise to game in hearts. Many South players would have rebid 6♡ immediately. The scoring table provides no bonuses for short auctions and we admire South's discipline in checking that the ace and king of trumps were not missing! How would you play this slam when West leads the ♣J?

At your local club there are no doubt plenty of players who would take the spade finesse. There is no need to rely on this chance immediately. After winning the club lead you should draw trumps in three rounds, ending in the dummy. You then play the ♣K, throwing a diamond from your hand. The time has come to play ace, king and another diamond.

If East wins the third diamond or the diamonds do not break 3-2, you will have to take the spade finesse. When the cards lie as in the diagram, West will win the third diamond and will be end-played. He will have to lead away from the ♠K or concede a ruff-and-discard. Since you have a further discard to come on dummy's fourth diamond, you will make the contract in either case.

On the next deal, played by Simon Cochemé at London's Young Chelsea Club, two differ-

> **TOP TIP**
>
> In an elimination situation, with trumps left in both hands, look for a suit such as A-K-x opposite 10-x-x, or A-K-x-x opposite x-x-x-x. When you cash the ace and king and exit in the suit, it may be that only one defender can win the lead. He may then have to lead into a tenace elsewhere, or give a ruff-and-discard.

ent elimination plays were possible. Declarer needed to count the hand in order to discover which of them had a chance of success.

Love all
Dealer North

```
                  ♠ A 9 3
                  ♡ K 5 4
                  ◇ 10 7 4
                  ♣ A J 8 2
   ♠ 7 6                        ♠ K 4
   ♡ 10 8 7 6 2        N        ♡ 9 3
   ◇ A 9           W       E    ◇ K Q J 8 6 5 2
   ♣ K 9 6 3           S        ♣ Q 10
                  ♠ Q J 10 8 5 2
                  ♡ A Q J
                  ◇ 3
                  ♣ 7 5 4
```

WEST	NORTH	EAST	SOUTH
-	1NT (12-14)	3◇	4♠
All Pass			

West opened the defence with ace and another diamond, declarer ruffing the second round. The trump queen was run to the king and East returned another diamond. Declarer ruffed high and West showed out. A trump to the ace drew the outstanding trumps. How would you continue?

Cochemé aimed for an elimination play. After removing the red suits he would throw East on lead with a club, forcing him to give a ruff-and-discard. All depended on how many clubs East held. If he had a singleton club, he could be end-played by leading a club towards the dummy and covering West's spot-card. Either dummy's card would win or East would capture with his singleton and would have to return a diamond, giving a ruff-and-discard. If instead East held two clubs, the best chance would be to cash the ace of clubs and attempt to end-play him on the second round.

When Cochemé played off the heart winners, East followed only twice. His shape was then known to be 2-2-7-2. Declarer duly played ace and another club and when East won the second round he had to concede the contract. East could not assist his cause by unblocking the queen of clubs. Declarer would then have a choice of plays: he could exit with a second club immediately, or cross to hand with a third trump and lead towards the ♣J. With East's second club being the ten, both lines would succeed.

Card reading is needed on the next deal, too. Fortunately both the opponents have bid and this will aid your task

> **TOP TIP**
>
> The best play in a key suit often depends on a complete count of the hand. In such a situation you should play on the other side suits to see how they lie, before tackling the key suit. When you have a two-way queen guess, for example, try to determine which defender started with more cards in the suit. He will then be favourite to hold the missing queen.

Game all
Dealer West

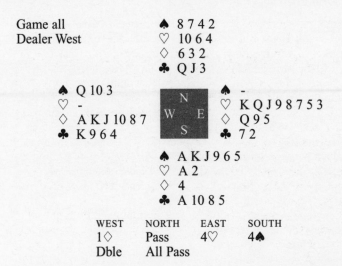

♠ 8 7 4 2
♡ 10 6 4
◇ 6 3 2
♣ Q J 3

♠ Q 10 3
♡ -
◇ A K J 10 8 7
♣ K 9 6 4

♠ -
♡ K Q J 9 8 7 5 3
◇ Q 9 5
♣ 7 2

♠ A K J 9 6 5
♡ A 2
◇ 4
♣ A 10 8 5

WEST	NORTH	EAST	SOUTH
1◇	Pass	4♡	4♠
Dble	All Pass		

West leads the ◇K and you ruff the diamond continuation.
The trump ace reveals the expected 3-0 break. What now?

West appears to be void in hearts and would not have doubled
you on the strength of one trump trick and a string of diamonds.
You should therefore place him with the club king and abandon
any thoughts of fighting your way to dummy to take a club finesse.

At Trick 4 you should lead a low club from your hand. West
will probably rise with the king and force you with another
diamond. If not, you can win the club trick in dummy and take
another diamond ruff yourself. However West chooses to defend,
you will soon reach this position:

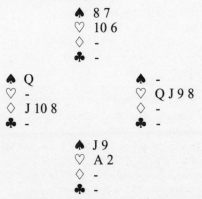

♠ 8 7
♡ 10 6
◇ -
♣ -

♠ Q
♡ -
◇ J 10 8
♣ -

♠ -
♡ Q J 9 8
◇ -
♣ -

♠ J 9
♡ A 2
◇ -
♣ -

You play the ♡A. If West ruffs, he will have to give you a ruff-and-discard. If instead he discards on the heart you will throw him in with a trump on the next trick with the same result.

Does anything else occur to you about that deal? East-West were cold for eleven tricks in hearts and even in diamonds. West could hardly be faulted for his double of 4♠. It was East, with his secondary fit for partner's diamonds, who might have bid to the five-level.

Declarer played well on our next ruff-and-discard elimination but the defenders had a chance to break the contract.

> **TOP TIP**
>
> When one defender has pre-empted and his partner does not lead the suit against your eventual trump contract, it is a fair bet that he is void in the suit. On this particular deal East could easily have bid 4♡ on a seven-card suit. The lack of a heart lead, or switch, strongly suggested that East had eight hearts.

North-South game
Dealer South

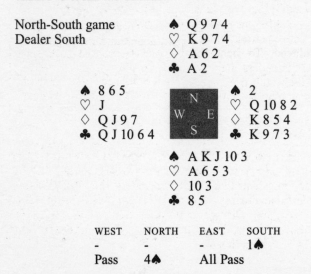

```
                    ♠ Q 9 7 4
                    ♡ K 9 7 4
                    ◇ A 6 2
                    ♣ A 2
        ♠ 8 6 5              ♠ 2
        ♡ J           N      ♡ Q 10 8 2
        ◇ Q J 9 7   W   E    ◇ K 8 5 4
        ♣ Q J 10 6 4   S     ♣ K 9 7 3
                    ♠ A K J 10 3
                    ♡ A 6 5 3
                    ◇ 10 3
                    ♣ 8 5
```

WEST	NORTH	EAST	SOUTH
-	-	-	1♠
Pass	4♠	All Pass	

Declarer won the ♣Q lead with the ace and drew trumps in three rounds, ending in the dummy. When he played a low diamond to the ten, West won with the jack and cashed a club winner. Declarer won the ◇Q exit with the ace and ruffed dummy's last diamond, completing the elimination of the minor suits. He then led a low heart from his hand, ducking when the jack appeared from West.

There was nothing the defenders could do at this stage. If West was left on lead he would have to concede a ruff-and-discard. If instead East overtook with the queen of hearts, he would either have to lead from the ten of hearts, allowing dummy's nine to score, or concede a ruff-and-discard himself.

How could the defenders have prevented this? West should have diagnosed from declarer's play of the diamond suit that he was aiming for an elimination ending. The key point in the defence came after West had cashed the club winner. At this moment he had to lead the ♡J, disembarrassing himself of the dangerous singleton honour. This would prevent any subsequent end-play.

Perhaps you are saying to yourself: 'I would have avoided any problem by leading the ♡J at Trick 1.' This does not break the contract, in fact. Declarer can draw trumps, duck a diamond, eliminate diamonds and exit on the second round of clubs. It makes no difference which defender wins the trick; he will be end-played. To beat the game the defenders have to establish their club trick, cash it and then play a round of hearts. Not easy!

> **TOP TIP**
>
> When a ruff-and-discard elimination is threatened, it is dangerous for a defender to hold a singleton honour in a side suit (sometimes even in the trump suit). You should consider leading such a card earlier in the play to avoid the risk of being thrown in with it.

We will end our section on the ruff-and-discard elimination with a reminiscence on one of Britain's all-time great players, Maurice Harrison-Gray. Two days before his death he discharged himself from hospital, against his doctor's orders, to partner Martin in a teams event at the Muswell Hill Bridge Club in North London. Despite conceding more than one 1100 penalty, Martin recalls, they still managed to win the event. Gray displayed his skill on this deal:

North-South game
Dealer South

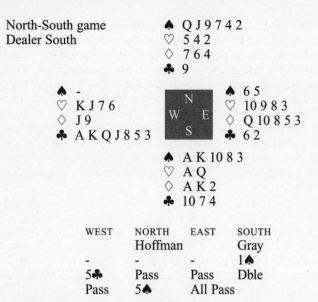

♠ Q J 9 7 4 2
♡ 5 4 2
◇ 7 6 4
♣ 9

♠ -
♡ K J 7 6
◇ J 9
♣ A K Q J 8 5 3

♠ 6 5
♡ 10 9 8 3
◇ Q 10 8 5 3
♣ 6 2

♠ A K 10 8 3
♡ A Q
◇ A K 2
♣ 10 7 4

WEST	NORTH	EAST	SOUTH
	Hoffman		Gray
-	-	-	1♠
5♣	Pass	Pass	Dble
Pass	5♠	All Pass	

West led out two top clubs against 5♠. Suppose you had held Gray's cards. How would you have played the contract?

Gray ruffed the second club and drew trumps in two rounds. A possible line was to ruff the last club and play ace, king and another diamond. If West won the third round he would have to lead into the heart tenace or give a ruff-and-discard.

Delaying his decision as to how to play the hand, Gray cashed the ace and king of diamonds without first ruffing his last club. West followed with the nine and jack. Was it possible that West had started with the ♡K-x-x and ◇Q-J-9? The risk of an end-play would have been obvious and he would surely have unblocked the queen and jack of diamonds, hoping his partner could win the third diamond with the ten.

Gray backed his judgement in the matter by switching to a different line of play. He led the ♣10 and discarded dummy's last diamond. Since West had indeed started with only two diamonds he was end-played in a different way from declarer's

> **TOP TIP**
>
> When a defender has shown great length in a suit, you can sometimes strip his holdings in the other suits and throw him in with your last card in his long suit. You discard a loser from the opposite hand. The benefit comes on the next trick, when the defender must give you a ruff-and-discard.

original intention. If only we could all end our bridge careers with such a well played hand!

We move now to the type of throw-in where no ruff-and-discard element is present. It is a potentially difficult play to execute because you may have to read the exact distribution. With most ruff-and-discard eliminations, you couldn't care less how the cards lie. You know that the defender thrown on lead will have to give you a trick anyway.

There is no problem in reading the cards on our first example:

North-South game
Dealer East

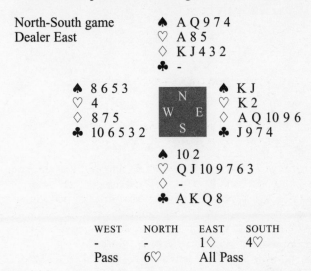

North
♠ A Q 9 7 4
♡ A 8 5
♢ K J 4 3 2
♣ -

West
♠ 8 6 5 3
♡ 4
♢ 8 7 5
♣ 10 6 5 3 2

East
♠ K J
♡ K 2
♢ A Q 10 9 6
♣ J 9 7 4

South
♠ 10 2
♡ Q J 10 9 7 6 3
♢ -
♣ A K Q 8

WEST	NORTH	EAST	SOUTH
-	-	1♢	4♡
Pass	6♡	All Pass	

TOP TIP

With K-x-x trumps missing, the percentage play is to finesse. When you can prepare an elimination ending, you may fare better by playing the ace first. You gain when the king drops singleton offside. You succeed also when the defender who wins the second round has to surrender a trick with his return. This play is particularly indicated when the defender sitting over the ace has bid and you suspect he holds the king.

A vulnerable 4♡ overcall deserves respect, yes, but North was pressing his luck going straight to six with those diamonds. A spade lead would have been lethal but West started with a diamond. Take the South cards now. How would you play the slam?

Declarer ruffed and advanced the queen of trumps. East's opening bid made it likely that the trump king was offside. When no cover came, declarer overtook with dummy's ace. East followed but the king did not drop. The aim now was to throw East on lead at a time when he would have no safe return. Declarer returned to hand with a diamond ruff and cashed the three top clubs. He then ruffed his last club, knowing that East would be in trouble if he overruffed. As the cards lay, East followed to the fourth club. Declarer played dummy's last trump to East's king and had his slam on any return. No ruff-and-discard element was necessary, since East could not safely play a spade or a diamond anyway.

The next deal is slightly more tricky:

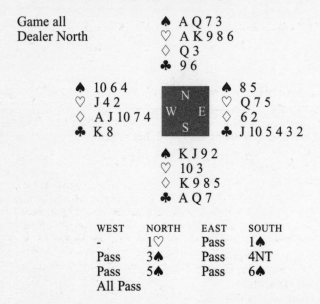

Game all   ♠ A Q 7 3
Dealer North ♡ A K 9 8 6
             ◇ Q 3
             ♣ 9 6

♠ 10 6 4   ♠ 8 5
♡ J 4 2   ♡ Q 7 5
◇ A J 10 7 4   ◇ 6 2
♣ K 8   ♣ J 10 5 4 3 2

             ♠ K J 9 2
             ♡ 10 3
             ◇ K 9 8 5
             ♣ A Q 7

WEST	NORTH	EAST	SOUTH
-	1♡	Pass	1♠
Pass	3♠	Pass	4NT
Pass	5♣	Pass	6♠
All Pass			

Declarer won the trump lead with the nine, played dummy's top hearts and ruffed a heart high, the suit breaking 3-3. After two more rounds of trumps, he played a diamond to the queen, which held. Take the South cards now. How will you continue?

One straightforward chance is to take the club finesse. If, for some reason, you think that West holds the ♣K you can cash dummy's major-suit winners, reducing your own hand to ◇K ♣A-Q. If West comes down to ◇A ♣K-x, you can throw him in with a diamond to lead into your club tenace. This is not particularly attractive because a skilled West may reduce to ◇A-7 ♣K (deceiving you by throwing the jack and ten of diamonds away). If you proceed with the intended throw-in then, West will score two diamond tricks. Can you see anything better?

This is the position at the moment:

```
              ♠ 7
              ♡ 9 8
              ◇ 3
              ♣ 9 6

    ♠ -                    ♠ -
    ♡ -                    ♡ -
    ◇ A J 10 7             ◇ 6
    ♣ K 8                  ♣ J 10 5 4 3

              ♠ -
              ♡ -
              ◇ K 9 8
              ♣ A Q 7
```

All you need to do now is to play a diamond to the nine! West wins and he must give you a trick with his return.

Suppose East had started with a doubleton jack or ten in the diamond suit and this card appeared on the second round, covered by the king and ace. You would then have a difficult guess to make when West returned a low diamond. The Principle of Restricted Choice would make West a favourite to hold the other middle diamond honour, so if all depended on the diamond guess you would run the return to your nine.

However, ruffing the diamond

> **TOP TIP**
>
> The Principle of Restricted Choice states that a defender is more likely to play a card because he is forced to than because he chooses it from equals. Suppose you hold A-K-x in your hand and Q-9-x-x in dummy. You cash the ace and king and right-hand-opponent follows with the jack or 10 on the second round. This card is twice as likely to be a singleton as a chosen card from J-10. You should therefore finesse the 9 next.

return in dummy gives you two chances — that the other middle diamond will fall from East or that the club finesse is right. In the case where running the diamond would work, clubs would have started 2-6 and the club finesse would be a '3-1 on' favourite. We saw some similar deals in the chapter on combining your options. The best line is to combine the second-best play in diamonds with the residual chance in clubs.

The next deal comes from a teams-of-four match contested on the Internet. (All eight players were in their own homes, in various countries, sitting at a computer screen.) At one table the bidding by the two defenders paved the way for a testing defence. Declarer might have survived, had he himself used the information provided by the auction.

Love all
Dealer West

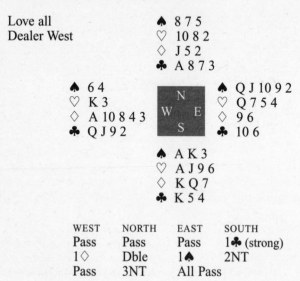

```
              ♠ 8 7 5
              ♡ 10 8 2
              ◇ J 5 2
              ♣ A 8 7 3
♠ 6 4                        ♠ Q J 10 9 2
♡ K 3             N          ♡ Q 7 5 4
◇ A 10 8 4 3   W   E         ◇ 9 6
♣ Q J 9 2         S          ♣ 10 6
              ♠ A K 3
              ♡ A J 9 6
              ◇ K Q 7
              ♣ K 5 4
```

WEST	NORTH	EAST	SOUTH
Pass	Pass	Pass	1♣ (strong)
1◇	Dble	1♠	2NT
Pass	3NT	All Pass	

At the other table West had led a diamond against 3NT. Declarer rose with dummy's jack and was able to take two heart finesses for the contract. Here West was guided by his partner's bid to lead a spade. Declarer won the first trick with the king, crossed to dummy with the ♣A and played a heart to the jack and king. When West led his remaining spade, declarer won with the ace and attempted to steal an entry to dummy by leading the ◇7. West peered at his computer screen for a second or two and then rose with the ace. The contract could no longer be made. Would you have done any better?

The best line is to cash both spade honours and then to play king and another club. If the queen should happen to appear from West (possibly from Q-x-x) you will duck. Otherwise win with dummy's ♣A and play a heart to the jack. West wins with the king and, as the cards lie, can cash two winners in clubs. He must then assist you with his next play. Whether he exits with a heart or a diamond, you will gain entry to the dummy and can score three heart tricks. Two diamond tricks will eventually bring your total to nine. The throw-in forces West to give you an entry, rather than a trick.

We will end the chapter with a fine piece of technique from Scottish ace, Victor Silverstone, partnering Martin in the Hoechst tournament in Amsterdam.

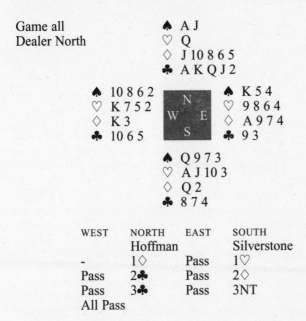

Game all
Dealer North

♠ A J
♡ Q
♢ J 10 8 6 5
♣ A K Q J 2

♠ 10 8 6 2
♡ K 7 5 2
♢ K 3
♣ 10 6 5

♠ K 5 4
♡ 9 8 6 4
♢ A 9 7 4
♣ 9 3

♠ Q 9 7 3
♡ A J 10 3
♢ Q 2
♣ 8 7 4

WEST	NORTH	EAST	SOUTH
	Hoffman		Silverstone
-	1♢	Pass	1♡
Pass	2♣	Pass	2♢
Pass	3♣	Pass	3NT
All Pass			

At both tables of the match a spade was led, dummy's jack losing to the king. The ♡9 switch went to West's king and a second round of spades was won with dummy's bare ace. How would you have continued as South?

Let's see first how the declarer at the other table went down. He played a diamond to the queen at Trick 4. West won with the king and exited with a second diamond, the jack in dummy holding the trick. With no entry to his hand, declarer could not avoid the loss of two further diamond tricks. He ended one down.

Silverstone set out to end-play one or other defender. Instead of playing on diamonds straight away, he cashed five rounds of clubs, discarding the ♠9 and one of his heart winners. These cards remained:

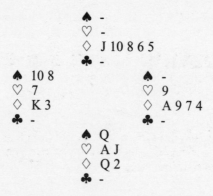

```
              ♠ -
              ♡ -
              ◇ J 10 8 6 5
              ♣ -
  ♠ 10 8              ♠ -
  ♡ 7                 ♡ 9
  ◇ K 3               ◇ A 9 7 4
  ♣ -                 ♣ -
              ♠ Q
              ♡ A J
              ◇ Q 2
              ♣ -
```

A diamond to the queen at this stage and Silverstone would have suffered the same fate as declarer at the other table. Instead he made the simple but brilliant play of the jack of diamonds. This ran to the king and West had to return another diamond, to avoid giving access to the major-suit winners in the South hand. When East won the second round of diamonds with the ace, he had to concede the last three tricks either to the South hand or to the dummy.

If East had started with a doubleton honour in diamonds, declarer could have avoided any guesswork in the end position by leading a low diamond from dummy instead of the jack. Silverstone placed West with seven black cards to East's five, so it was unlikely that West would have two more diamonds than his partner.

TOP TIP

Suppose you know the lie of two suits already and one defender has turned up with more than half the outstanding cards there. When you come to make the key play in a different suit you should assume the length will lie with the other defender. This may seem obvious if you are already familiar with the technique of 'counting the hand'. The vast majority of the world's bridge players go to their graves without ever achieving this feat!

4
Preparing for a Squeeze

To get you into the right frame of mind for this chapter, let's start with a technical hand that involves several common preparatory moves leading to a squeeze.

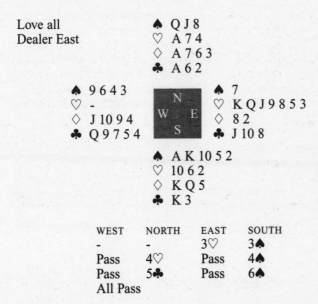

Love all
Dealer East

```
                    ♠ Q J 8
                    ♡ A 7 4
                    ◇ A 7 6 3
                    ♣ A 6 2
  ♠ 9 6 4 3                          ♠ 7
  ♡ -               N                ♡ K Q J 9 8 5 3
  ◇ J 10 9 4      W   E              ◇ 8 2
  ♣ Q 9 7 5 4       S                ♣ J 10 8
                    ♠ A K 10 5 2
                    ♡ 10 6 2
                    ◇ K Q 5
                    ♣ K 3
```

WEST	NORTH	EAST	SOUTH
-	-	3♡	3♠
Pass	4♡	Pass	4♠
Pass	5♣	Pass	6♠
All Pass			

You win the ◇J lead in the South hand, already visualising that dummy's diamonds may provide a threat in some squeeze ending. You draw trumps in four rounds, discarding a heart from dummy. East, meanwhile, throws three hearts. What next?

To make a small slam on a squeeze it is generally necessary to surrender a trick first — to 'rectify the count', as it is called. This removes a spare card from the defenders' hands, tightening the eventual end position. Here you can afford to duck a heart. You win East's club return with the king and these cards remain:

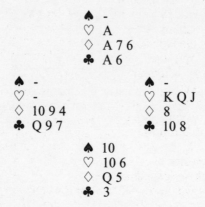

The general idea now is that West holds the diamond guard, East holds the heart guard, so no-one will be able to hold on to two clubs when you cash the last trump. However, if you play the last trump now neither West nor East will come under any pressure.

Two further preparatory steps are necessary. The first is to cash the ♡A. This play, known as a Vienna Coup, frees the ♡10 to act as a threat. The next step is to cash the ace and queen of diamonds. Unless you do this, East will not be put under any pressure by the last spade. This is the much improved end position:

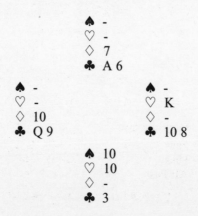

The moment has come to play the last spade. West has to throw a club to keep his diamond guard. You release the ◇7 from dummy and East has to throw a club to retain his heart guard. You then score two club tricks in dummy to rack up the slam.

An experienced squeeze practitioner would visualise the three-card end position as early as Trick 1. East has shown long hearts by his bid and West has suggested long

> **TOP TIP**
>
> All squeezes need a one-card threat and a two-card threat containing an entry. Suppose in one suit you have the A-x in dummy and Q-x in your hand. If this is your intended two-card threat, you must play the squeeze-card while the ace is still in position. If instead you have a two-card threat elsewhere and intend to use the queen as the one-card threat, it will usually be right to cash the ace that lies opposite. This will prevent the suit becoming blocked.

diamonds by his lead. All the other cards in the pack (in particular the ♡A and the ◇A-Q) are mere clutter that must be removed before the squeeze can operate.

An opposing overcall placed the cards for declarer on the next deal but it was not so easy to foresee the eventual squeeze position.

```
North-South game        ♠ A J 4
Dealer South            ♡ A K Q 5 3
                        ◇ 10 4 2
                        ♣ J 2

        ♠ 8 2              N          ♠ 9 7 3
        ♡ 2          W         E      ♡ J 10 9 8 6 4
        ◇ Q J 9 8 7        S         ◇ A 5 3
        ♣ Q 9 7 5 3                   ♣ 4

                        ♠ K Q 10 6 5
                        ♡ 7
                        ◇ K 6
                        ♣ A K 10 8 6
```

WEST	NORTH	EAST	SOUTH
-	-	-	1♠
2NT (1)	3♡	Pass	3NT
Pass	4♠	Pass	4NT
Pass	5♡	Pass	6♠
All Pass			

(1) Unusual No-trump, promising both minor suits.

After North's bid in hearts West spurned the lead of his singleton and opened with the ◇Q. East won with the ace and returned the ♡J. How would you play the hand from this point?

You have eleven top tricks and know from West's 2NT overcall that he holds the sole guard on both minors. If East had made any return but a heart you could have played five rounds of trumps, followed by the ◇K (if not already removed) and three rounds of hearts. West would then have no good discard. East's heart return has made life awkward. You need to be in dummy when you play the squeeze card (to have access to the ◇10, should West choose to unguard that suit). What can be done?

The answer is somewhat unusual. You must ruff two hearts in the South hand! Once your two surplus trumps are out of the way you can draw trumps, ending in the dummy. You can then play the remaining two hearts to effect the squeeze.

How does the play go? You ruff a low heart with the ♠10 at Trick 3 and play the king and jack of trumps. You then ruff another heart with the queen. The king of diamonds is followed by a trump to dummy's ace, providing access to dummy's remaining heart winners. You cash one of these to leave this position:

When you play the ♡Q, West is left with no good discard.

If West leads the ♡2 against the slam, the play is interesting again. You win with the ace and ruff a heart high, West throwing a diamond. When you draw trumps, ending in the dummy, West cannot reduce his club guard and has to throw another diamond. You then play the ♡K-Q, discarding both your diamonds. West has to part with yet another diamond and these cards remain:

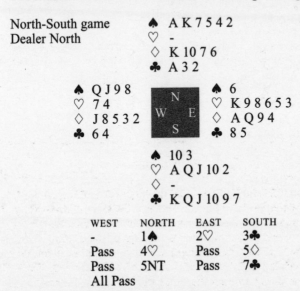

```
              ♠ -
              ♡ 5
              ◇ 10 4 2
              ♣ J 2

  ♠ -                    ♠ -
  ♡ -                    ♡ J 10
  ◇ Q                    ◇ A 5 3
  ♣ Q 9 7 5 3            ♣ 4

              ♠ 10
              ♡ -
              ◇ -
              ♣ A K 10 8 6
```

You ruff a diamond to remove West's last card in the suit and lead a low club towards dummy. If West goes in with the queen, you will unblock dummy's jack to leave West end-played. If instead West plays low, you will win with dummy's ♣J and play a club to the eight or ten, again end-playing West. It is a form of 'squeeze without the count' (a play we will look at again in Chapter 8). You concede a trick after the squeeze has taken effect.

On the next deal success depends on an error by a defender. The situation is one where defenders often do go wrong, however.

North-South game · Dealer North

```
                   ♠ A K 7 5 4 2
                   ♡ -
                   ◇ K 10 7 6
                   ♣ A 3 2

  ♠ Q J 9 8                        ♠ 6
  ♡ 7 4            N               ♡ K 9 8 6 5 3
  ◇ J 8 5 3 2    W   E             ◇ A Q 9 4
  ♣ 6 4            S               ♣ 8 5

                   ♠ 10 3
                   ♡ A Q J 10 2
                   ◇ -
                   ♣ K Q J 10 9 7
```

WEST	NORTH	EAST	SOUTH
-	1♠	2♡	3♣
Pass	4♡	Pass	5◇
Pass	5NT	Pass	7♣
All Pass			

Perhaps you guessed from North's ambitious efforts in the auction that it was Martin in that seat! West led the ♡7 and when declarer discarded a diamond from dummy, East was too smart to put in the king. Declarer won with the queen and took the simple line of drawing two rounds of trumps and playing for a 3-2 spade break. Not today! Can you see a better line? One, perhaps, that will give the defenders a chance to go wrong?

There is no future in ruffing three hearts. East must have at least six hearts for his overcall on a king-high suit. When you take your second ruff, West will be able to insert a trump spot-card to force dummy's ace. He will then be able to ruff the next heart in front of the dummy.

Martin's suggestion to his partner was to cross to the ace of spades at Trick 2 and to lead a low diamond from dummy. This type of play will frequently draw an indiscretion from the defender on your right. If his holding is headed by the ace-jack, he may rise with the ace, fearing that you hold a singleton queen. Here he may place you with a singleton jack and insert the queen. This may look like no big gain but it will allow you to make the contract!

You ruff the queen of diamonds, ruff a heart in dummy and then lead the king of diamonds, which East has to cover. After ruffing the second round of diamonds, you ruff another heart with the ace and run the trump suit. Because the diamond guard has been transferred to West, he will be squeezed in spades and diamonds by the last trump.

Suppose, after this start to the play, that East held the spade guard instead. The last

> ### TOP TIP
>
> You can gain many an extra trick by leading a low card from dummy, applying pressure on your right-hand defender. Suppose you hold A-Q-x-x in dummy and 8-x-x-x in your hand. Lead low from dummy on the first round! There are plenty of defenders around who will help you by going in with the king from K-x. Give them a chance to go wrong. If instead you take a mundane first-round finesse of the queen, the defender is not posed any problem.

trump would then squeeze him in the majors. The technique is known as 'playing a simple squeeze as a double squeeze'. One or other defender will be squeezed and you don't mind which.

The next deal, a difficult one, arose in a Rosenblum match between teams from Israel and Great Britain.

East-West game
Dealer South

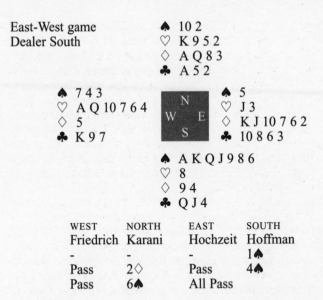

```
                  ♠ 10 2
                  ♡ K 9 5 2
                  ◇ A Q 8 3
                  ♣ A 5 2

  ♠ 7 4 3                        ♠ 5
  ♡ A Q 10 7 6 4    N           ♡ J 3
  ◇ 5            W     E         ◇ K J 10 7 6 2
  ♣ K 9 7           S           ♣ 10 8 6 3

                  ♠ A K Q J 9 8 6
                  ♡ 8
                  ◇ 9 4
                  ♣ Q J 4
```

WEST	NORTH	EAST	SOUTH
Friedrich	Karani	Hochzeit	Hoffman
-	-	-	1♠
Pass	2◇	Pass	4♠
Pass	6♠	All Pass	

West led the ace of hearts and continued with the heart queen. How would you have played the slam?

To have any chance of success you will need West to hold the ♣K. It was likely that he held six hearts to the ace-queen to justify his opening lead (he was no doubt hoping to give his partner a ruff). West could hardly hold the diamond king in addition or he would have entered the auction. What can be done if the ◇K is offside, as you fear?

One chance is to discard a diamond on the ♡K and play to bring down the diamond king with two ruffs. This is not very

> **TOP TIP**
>
> An opponent shows up with a good suit but he failed to overcall. Ask yourself why. In all likelihood his partner will hold the high cards that are outstanding. When, as declarer, you are reconstructing the defenders' hands, you must always think back to the bidding and check that your reading of the cards matches the defenders' action (or lack of action) at that stage.

likely since West is marked with heart length and East is therefore likely to be long in diamonds. The winning line is to ruff the second round of hearts, leaving dummy's ♡K intact. You then cross to dummy's ◇A, a Vienna Coup to set up your ◇9 as an unhindered threat. Finally you run six rounds of trumps. The squeeze is a difficult one to foresee but this is the end position:

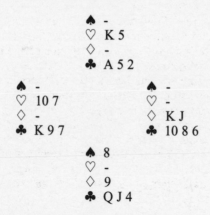

```
        ♠ -
        ♡ K 5
        ◇ -
        ♣ A 5 2
♠ -              ♠ -
♡ 10 7           ♡ -
◇ -              ◇ K J
♣ K 9 7          ♣ 10 8 6
        ♠ 8
        ♡ -
        ◇ 9
        ♣ Q J 4
```

When the last trump is played, West has to retain his heart holding and must therefore reduce his guard on the club king. Dummy's ♡5 can be thrown now and East discards the jack of diamonds. Declarer next plays the queen of clubs. West has only two clubs left and cannot afford to let the queen pass or declarer will score three club tricks. The queen is covered by the king and ace and declarer now plays dummy's ♡K to squeeze East in the minors. It's amazing how precious South's ◇9 turned out to be.

A squeeze seems easy on the next deal, but only an unusual line of play is good enough. See what you make of it.

North-South game
Dealer East

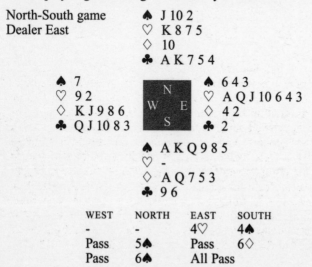

```
                    ♠ J 10 2
                    ♡ K 8 7 5
                    ◇ 10
                    ♣ A K 7 5 4
♠ 7                              ♠ 6 4 3
♡ 9 2                            ♡ A Q J 10 6 4 3
◇ K J 9 8 6                      ◇ 4 2
♣ Q J 10 8 3                     ♣ 2
                    ♠ A K Q 9 8 5
                    ♡ -
                    ◇ A Q 7 5 3
                    ♣ 9 6
```

WEST	NORTH	EAST	SOUTH
-	-	4♡	4♠
Pass	5♣	Pass	6◇
Pass	6♠	All Pass	

North's 5♠ asked South for a heart control and South's 6◇ response showed controls in both red suits, suggesting a grand slam. Everything would have been easy on a club lead. Declarer could take three diamond ruffs and in fact score all thirteen tricks by squeezing West in the minors. Defenders sometimes do annoying things and here West did just that by leading a trump. How would you have played the spade slam then?

Declarer won the trump lead in his hand, cashed the ◇A and ruffed a diamond. A heart ruff was followed by a second diamond ruff, with dummy's last trump. Declarer re-entered his hand with a second heart ruff and drew East's outstanding trumps. One trick short, he now turned his mind towards a minor-suit squeeze on West. These cards remained:

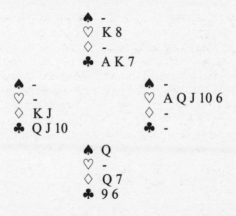

The count had not been rectified and it would do declarer no good to play the last trump at this stage. West would simply discard the ◇J. Although declarer could then set up the ◇Q by ducking a round of the suit, there would be no entry to enjoy the card. Declarer tried something different. He crossed to the ♣A and played a heart. East won the trick and declarer threw a diamond from his hand. West, not yet in trouble, also had to throw a diamond. When East returned another round of hearts, declarer ruffed with the queen and West was (at last!) squeezed. If he threw the ◇K, South's ◇Q would score; if instead he threw a club, dummy would score an extra club trick. The play is known as a suicide squeeze because a defender leads the squeeze card, thereby inflicting damage on his own side.

Here is another example of the suicide squeeze. The deal was played by Brian Senior, who has the distinction of representing both England and Ireland in internationals.

Game all
Dealer South

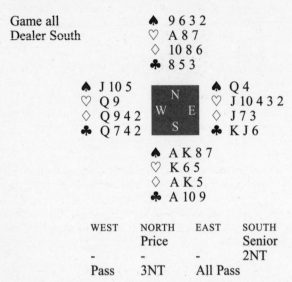

```
                    ♠ 9 6 3 2
                    ♡ A 8 7
                    ◇ 10 8 6
                    ♣ 8 5 3
  ♠ J 10 5                          ♠ Q 4
  ♡ Q 9              N              ♡ J 10 4 3 2
  ◇ Q 9 4 2      W       E          ◇ J 7 3
  ♣ Q 7 4 2          S              ♣ K J 6
                    ♠ A K 8 7
                    ♡ K 6 5
                    ◇ A K 5
                    ♣ A 10 9
```

WEST	NORTH	EAST	SOUTH
	Price		Senior
-	-	-	2NT
Pass	3NT	All Pass	

West started with the ◇2 and East topped dummy's ten with the jack. Senior allowed this card to win and captured the diamond continuation. His next move was to play the ace of spades. If a singleton honour had fallen from West, three spade tricks could be made by continuing with a low spade, setting up a third-round finesse. Two lowly spot-cards appeared and Senior ducked a spade to set up the suit. East won and cleared the diamond suit. Would you have seen any chance at this stage?

Prospects were poor indeed against best defence but Senior was not willing to give up. He played two more spades, ending in the dummy. A club to the ten left West on lead with these cards still to be played:

```
              ♠ -
              ♡ A 8 7
              ◇ -
              ♣ 8 5

♠ -                          ♠ -
♡ Q 9        ┌───────┐       ♡ J 10 4
◇ Q          │ N     │       ◇ -
♣ 7 4        │ W   E │       ♣ K J
             │   S   │
             └───────┘
              ♠ -
              ♡ K 6 5
              ◇ -
              ♣ A 9
```

A heart or a club from West now would defeat the game. West did what most defenders would do and cashed his ◇Q. East was squeezed and had to surrender the game-going trick.

We'll end the chapter with a big-name declarer producing the goods — Andrew Robson. Here he is, playing in the Hoechst Tournament in Holland.

Love all   ♠ 7 5
Dealer South   ♡ A 10 9 8
                     ◇ A 8 7
                     ♣ A 8 6 3

```
♠ 4                          ♠ J 10 9 2
♡ Q J 7 3    ┌───────┐       ♡ -
◇ J 10 9 4 2 │ N     │       ◇ K Q 6 5 3
♣ J 5 4      │ W   E │       ♣ Q 9 7 2
             │   S   │
             └───────┘
```

                     ♠ A K Q 8 6 3
                     ♡ K 6 5 4 2
                     ◇ -
                     ♣ K 10

WEST	NORTH	EAST	SOUTH
	Segal		Robson
-	-	-	1♠
Pass	2♣	Pass	2♡
Pass	4◇	Dble	Rdble
Pass	4♡	Pass	5♣
Pass	6♡	All Pass	

West led the jack of diamonds, won in the dummy, and declarer threw a spade. If trumps broke 2-2 or 3-1, there would be a spare trump in dummy to deal with a 4-1 spade break. As a safety play against a 4-0 trump break on either side Robson called for dummy's ♡8. His intention was to run the card if East followed suit, guaranteeing no more than one trump loser. East in fact showed out. This was the first key moment of the hand. Would you have run the ♡8 nevertheless or won with the king?

At the other table declarer rose with the king of trumps and the contract could no longer be made. Robson chose to run the ♡8 and West returned another diamond, ruffed in the South hand. A trump to dummy's nine was followed by the king and ace of clubs and a club ruffed with the king. A low trump to the ten left the lead in dummy in this end position:

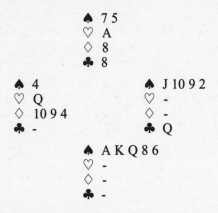

```
                    ♠ 7 5
                    ♡ A
                    ◇ 8
                    ♣ 8

        ♠ 4                      ♠ J 10 9 2
        ♡ Q                      ♡ -
        ◇ 10 9 4                 ◇ -
        ♣ -                      ♣ Q

                    ♠ A K Q 8 6
                    ♡ -
                    ◇ -
                    ♣ -
```

When Robson drew the last trump with dummy's ace, East was squeezed. He had to abandon his guard on one of the black suits and the small slam was made.

5

Avoiding Ruffs

As declarer, you have various techniques at your disposal to
reduce the risk of suffering an adverse ruff. One of the most
important of these is simple indeed — you lead towards an
honour, through the defender who has the potential to ruff. The
technique is needed on this deal:

North-South game
Dealer West

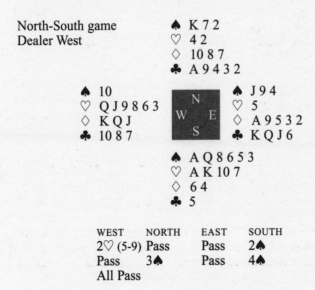

♠ K 7 2
♡ 4 2
◇ 10 8 7
♣ A 9 4 3 2

♠ 10
♡ Q J 9 8 6 3
◇ K Q J
♣ 10 8 7

♠ J 9 4
♡ 5
◇ A 9 5 3 2
♣ K Q J 6

♠ A Q 8 6 5 3
♡ A K 10 7
◇ 6 4
♣ 5

WEST	NORTH	EAST	SOUTH
2♡ (5-9)	Pass	Pass	2♠
Pass	3♠	Pass	4♠
All Pass			

West leads his diamond honours against the spade game and
you ruff the third round. How would you continue?

You need to ruff some hearts in the dummy and West's weak-
two opening makes it likely that East holds only one heart. The
winning play is to draw one round of trumps, cash the ♡A, and
cross to dummy with the ♣A to lead a second round of hearts
towards your hand.

If East ruffs a losing heart, it will be easy for you to ruff your only remaining loser in the suit. Let's suppose that he discards instead and your king of hearts wins the second round. What now? Ruffing a heart with the ♠7 is not much good. East will overruff and remove dummy's last trump. No, you must ruff your penultimate heart with the king. You can then return to hand with a club ruff to ruff your last heart with the seven. East is welcome to overruff, since you will lose just two diamond tricks and one trump trick.

TOP TIP

Suppose, playing a trump contract, you have a side suit of K-x-x in the dummy and A-Q-x-x in your hand. If you need to play on this suit before drawing all the adverse trumps, the best sequence may be ace, king and then low towards the queen. If your right-hand-opponent started with a doubleton, he can only ruff a loser. You may then be able to throw a card from dummy on the good queen of the first suit and take a ruff in the second suit. By leading towards an honour on the third round, you reduce the chance of having it ruffed.

Before we move on, did you spot that the defenders could have done better? Let's suppose they are playing a signalling method that is popular among Britain's top players, 'ace for attitude, king for count'. (This means that you signal attitude when partner leads an ace; you signal your count when he leads a king.) Here East would signal with the ♦2 on the opening lead. Declarer has long spades and is marked with some heart length after East's failure to raise the weak two. It is therefore almost certain from West's point of view that declarer has two diamonds to East's five. After cashing a second diamond, West could make a lethal switch to clubs. This would kill a key entry to dummy before declarer was ready to use it — to lead the second round of hearts. The contract would then go down.

Here is another example of the technique:

Game all
Dealer South

```
                    ♠ 7 3 2
                    ♡ 6 5 3
                    ◇ A 9 7 2
                    ♣ K Q 2
  ♠ 8                              ♠ J 10 9 6
  ♡ K 10 9 7         N             ♡ 8 4
  ◇ J 8 6 4      W       E         ◇ Q 10 3
  ♣ 10 9 8 5         S             ♣ A J 6 4
                    ♠ A K Q 5 4
                    ♡ A Q J 2
                    ◇ K 5
                    ♣ 7 3
```

WEST	NORTH	EAST	SOUTH
-	-	-	1♠
Pass	1NT	Pass	3♡
Pass	4♠	All Pass	

West led the ♣10, covered by the king and ace. The club return was won with dummy's queen and declarer played a heart to the queen and king. He ruffed the club continuation and drew two rounds of trumps. If trumps had broken 3-2, it would be safe to continue with the ♡J. Even if this card were ruffed, there would be a spare trump in dummy to ruff the fourth round of hearts.

When trumps actually broke 4-1 it was not safe to continue with the heart jack. East would ruff and would still be in a position to overruff on the fourth round of hearts. Instead declarer crossed to the ◇A and led a third round of hearts from dummy. East could not afford to ruff a loser with a natural trump trick and South's ♡J won the trick. Declarer ruffed his last heart in dummy and East could choose when he scored his trump trick. The defenders made just one heart, one club and a trump trick.

Did any other point occur to you on that last deal? It would be a difficult defence to find, but suppose West ducks smoothly when the queen of hearts is finessed. Declarer will doubtless cross to the ◇A

TOP TIP

When declarer finesses an A-Q-J combination, it is often worthwhile to refuse to win with the king on the first round. Declarer may waste an entry to repeat the finesse. He may also base his next play on the (false) assumption that the king is onside. The same is true when you hold an ace over a king-queen combination.

(the last entry to dummy) to repeat the heart finesse. When this loses, West must resist the temptation to give his partner a heart ruff. If instead he exits in either minor, declarer will no longer have the chance to lead the third round of hearts from dummy. One down!

Another way to prevent an unwanted ruff is to attack the defenders' communications. There are various techniques available. On the next deal declarer also needed some luck.

Game all   ♠ 7 6 4
Dealer North   ♡ A K Q 7 6 5 2
               ♢ Q
               ♣ 10 2

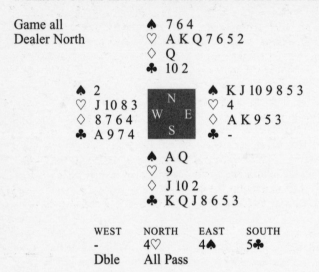

     ♠ 2   ♠ K J 10 9 8 5 3
     ♡ J 10 8 3   ♡ 4
     ♢ 8 7 6 4   ♢ A K 9 5 3
     ♣ A 9 7 4   ♣ -

               ♠ A Q
               ♡ 9
               ♢ J 10 2
               ♣ K Q J 8 6 5 3

WEST	NORTH	EAST	SOUTH
-	4♡	4♠	5♣
Dble	All Pass		

The pickings from 4♠ doubled would have been lean. Indeed, they would be non-existent if South chose to lead ♣K. South opted for the club game instead and West closed the auction with a double. How would you plan the play when West leads the ♠2?

Declarer could see his fate if he played a round of trumps. West would win and cross to his partner's hand with a diamond to receive a spade ruff. What could be done about it? This was one of the rare hands where declarer must hope for a 4-0 trump break! He crossed to the ace of hearts and continued with the heart king. East was out of hearts but could not ruff. Declarer threw one of his diamond losers on this trick and another on the heart queen.

The danger was not over and if declarer played on trumps at this stage he would still suffer a spade ruff. To cut the link between the defenders' hands he played a fourth round of hearts and threw his last diamond. West had to win the trick and the contract was secure.

Declarer ruffed the diamond switch and led a trump to the ten. West won the next round of trumps but could not prevent declarer from winning the return, drawing trumps and claiming the contract. It was an unusual example of the loser-on-loser technique known as the Scissors Coup. Declarer swapped one loser for another, thereby keeping the dangerous defender off lead.

On the next deal the risk was not an enemy ruff but a trump promotion. Declarer had no excuse for failing to address this threat because the bidding had warned him of a bad trump break.

> **TOP TIP**
>
> Suppose you are playing in a spade contract with a side suit of $\heartsuit$A-K-Q-x in the dummy opposite a singleton. You cash the three winners, throwing two losers from your hand. It is often good technique to play the last heart (a loser), throwing yet another loser from your own hand. There are two possible advantages to be gained. You may be able to throw a particular defender on lead — the one with the heart length. You may also avoid any risk of a trump promotion by the defenders playing a fourth heart themselves.

North-South game
Dealer North

	♠ K Q J	
	♡ A	
	◇ A 9 8 7 5	
	♣ 10 7 4 2	

♠ 8 6 3		♠ A 10 9 7 5 4
♡ Q 9 4 2	N	♡ 3
◇ K Q J 3	W E	◇ 10 6 4
♣ K 5	S	♣ Q J 9

	♠ 2	
	♡ K J 10 8 7 6 5	
	◇ 2	
	♣ A 8 6 3	

WEST	NORTH	EAST	SOUTH
-	1◇	1♠	4♡
Dble	All Pass		

Declarer won the ◇K lead with dummy's ace. Pleased to have

avoided a club lead, he knocked out the ace of spades. When the club queen was returned, declarer won with the ace and West unblocked the king. A trump to dummy's ace brought the welcome sight of East following suit. Declarer threw two club losers on the queen and jack of spades, reached his hand with a diamond ruff and then played the king and jack of trumps. West won with the trump queen and these cards remained:

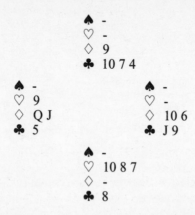

```
                    ♠ -
                    ♡ -
                    ◇ 9
                    ♣ 10 7 4

♠ -                              ♠ -
♡ 9                              ♡ -
◇ Q J                            ◇ 10 6
♣ 5                              ♣ J 9

                    ♠ -
                    ♡ 10 8 7
                    ◇ -
                    ♣ 8
```

West crossed to his partner's hand with a club and another club promoted the bare nine of trumps. That was one down.

How could declarer have avoided this gory fate? It was simple enough. He should have ducked the ♣Q switch. This would break the link between the defenders and prevent them from achieving a trump promotion. Declarer would score six trumps, two spades and the two minor-suit aces.

TOP TIP

If the defenders attack a suit where you hold A-x-x-x or A-x-x opposite x-x-x-x or x-x-x, it is often right to duck the first round. By doing so, you may kill the defenders' communications in the suit, perhaps preventing them from cashing their winners there.

On the next deal declarer went down in a slam, suffering an adverse ruff. Can you spot how he might have done better?

North-South game
Dealer East

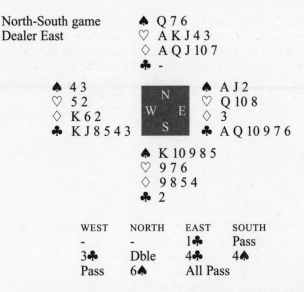

	♠ Q 7 6
	♡ A K J 4 3
	◇ A Q J 10 7
	♣ -

♠ 4 3	♠ A J 2
♡ 5 2	♡ Q 10 8
◇ K 6 2	◇ 3
♣ K J 8 5 4 3	♣ A Q 10 9 7 6

	♠ K 10 9 8 5
	♡ 9 7 6
	◇ 9 8 5 4
	♣ 2

WEST	NORTH	EAST	SOUTH
-	-	1♣	Pass
3♣	Dble	4♣	4♠
Pass	6♠	All Pass	

West led a club, ruffed low in the dummy, and declarer called for dummy's queen of trumps. All would have been well if East had captured this card. Declarer could have drawn trumps and finessed successfully in diamonds, eventually throwing his heart loser on the fifth round of the suit. East could see a good chance of beating the slam, however. He ducked the first round of trumps, won the second with the ace and returned his singleton diamond. Declarer tried his luck with the nine but West covered smartly with the king. Declarer was now locked in dummy and could not prevent East from scoring a diamond ruff. Any idea how to make the slam?

Suppose you ruff the club lead with dummy's queen of trumps. This costs little in terms of picking up the trump suit because you are committed to finessing East for the trump jack anyway. You continue with a low trump

> **TOP TIP**
>
> When entries to your hand are sparse, consider taking ruffs in the dummy with a higher trump than is necessary. This may promote the entry potential of the lesser trumps in your own hand.

from dummy and now the benefit from the play at Trick 1 emerges. When East ducks, you finesse the ten successfully and are conveniently in your hand. You play a diamond to the queen, which happens to remove East's holding in the suit. When a second trump is led, East wins with the ace but no longer has his singleton diamond as a means of locking you in the dummy. A low heart exit will be won by South's nine. If instead East plays the queen or ten of hearts, you will have to win in the dummy. Two more rounds of hearts will survive and you will then return to hand by ruffing the fourth round of hearts.

Playing in this fashion it is true that you have to guess whether East holds one diamond or two. (If two, you must cash the ◇A before playing a second round of trumps.) Whichever guess you take in respect of the diamonds, you are at least giving yourself an extra chance over the line originally chosen. One reason to play East for a singleton diamond is that if his shape were 3-2-2-6 he would be able to end-play the dummy with a heart.

We will end the chapter with a deal where declarer must employ one of three techniques, depending on how the defence goes. (Good value for your money!)

```
Game all              ♠ 4 2
Dealer South          ♡ 8 5 4
                      ◇ K Q J 9 7 5
                      ♣ 8 7

    ♠ K Q 10                      ♠ A J 9 8 7 5
    ♡ J 7 6 2        N            ♡ 10 3
    ◇ 8          W       E        ◇ 10 6 2
    ♣ Q J 9 5 2      S            ♣ 10 3

                      ♠ 6 3
                      ♡ A K Q 9
                      ◇ A 4 3
                      ♣ A K 6 4
```

WEST	NORTH	EAST	SOUTH
-	-	-	1♣
Pass	1◇	Pass	2♡
Pass	3◇	Pass	4◇
Pass	4♡	All Pass	

The diamond game would have been safer but North-South deserve some credit for not ending in 3NT. At the table West cashed the king and queen of spades and switched to the club queen. How would you play the contract after that start?

Suppose you win with the ♣A and play three rounds of trumps, finding that they break 4-2. When you turn to the diamond suit, West will delay his ruff until the third round. You will go two down. Nor will you succeed if you attempt to ruff two clubs, hoping that any overruff will absorb the defenders' potential trump trick. No, you should play the ace and nine of trumps, surrendering a trump trick when it is safe to do so. A third round of spades will not damage you then because you can ruff in the dummy. You will win the return, draw trumps, and run the diamonds.

Suppose next that West switches to the ◇8 after cashing two spades. What then?

> **TOP TIP**
>
> When you have the ability to ruff the enemy suit in the dummy, it is often beneficial to surrender an early round of trumps. Since dummy can still ruff, the defenders cannot then damage you by playing on their strong suit. If instead you attempt to draw trumps and run into a bad break, your protection in the enemy suit will be gone when the defenders score their trump trick.

If you play three rounds of trumps, you will suffer the fate we visualised above. To make the contract you must win the diamond switch in dummy and play a trump to the nine, ducking the trick to the safe hand. You would suffer a diamond ruff if West had started with three diamonds, it's true, but West is unlikely to have switched to the 8 from ◇10-8-6. In any case the risk of suffering a diamond ruff is less than that of a 4-2 trump break.

Finally, let's imagine that West switches to a diamond after cashing just one spade. How would you play the contract then?

You cannot duck a trump to West now, because he can cross to the East hand with a spade to receive his ruff. There is only one winning play. You win the diamond switch with the ace and, at Trick 3, play a spade yourself! East is welcome to win and give his partner a diamond ruff. You would then be able to draw trumps and run the diamonds. And if West declines to ruff the second round of diamonds, you will win in the dummy and only then play a heart to the nine. With the second spade out of the way West has become 'safe' again.

Did you spot the only defence that will succeed against the super-declarer? West must lead his diamond singleton at Trick 1.

6

Deception in Defence

The game of bridge brings many rewards but for some players the ultimate satisfaction is to make or break a contract by deception — by persuading an opponent that your hand is other than it is. In this chapter we will consider deception solely from the defenders' point of view

On the first deal declarer spotted an extra chance of making his contract. By the time the play was over, he wished that he hadn't!

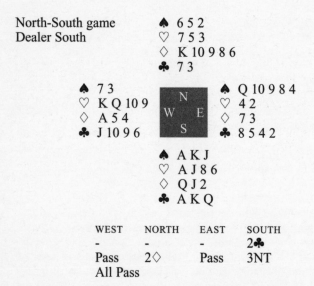

North-South game
Dealer South

♠ 6 5 2
♡ 7 5 3
◇ K 10 9 8 6
♣ 7 3

♠ 7 3
♡ K Q 10 9
◇ A 5 4
♣ J 10 9 6

♠ Q 10 9 8 4
♡ 4 2
◇ 7 3
♣ 8 5 4 2

♠ A K J
♡ A J 8 6
◇ Q J 2
♣ A K Q

WEST	NORTH	EAST	SOUTH
-	-	-	2♣
Pass	2◇	Pass	3NT
All Pass			

Declarer won the ♣J lead and saw that all would be easy if the ace of diamonds was singleton or doubleton. He would then be able to score four diamond tricks. If the ace of diamonds could be held up for two rounds, he would have only eight tricks at his disposal. He would then need to score an extra trick in one of the majors to bring the total to nine.

One obvious line was to play the queen of diamonds followed by the jack, overtaking with dummy's king. The defender with the ace would have to duck and it would then be possible to take a spade finesse. Declarer cast his eye on the heart suit. What were the prospects of an extra trick there? Suppose he ducked a heart, won the black-suit return and cashed the ace of hearts. If West had started with a doubleton honour it would fall under the ace and he could then use dummy's diamond entry to lead towards his ♡J-x. That line would succeed also if hearts were 3-3. If no heart honour fell under the ace nothing would have been lost. Should he wish, he could still use the diamond entry to take a spade finesse.

At Trick 2 declarer led the ♡6 from his hand. West won with the ten and returned a second round of clubs to the king. When declarer cashed a second round of hearts, West made the cost-nothing play of dropping the king! This appeared to be excellent news from South's point of view. Whether West had started with K-10 doubleton or K-Q-10 tripleton, it would be possible to set up an extra heart trick by leading towards the ♡J.

Declarer won the next trick with the queen of diamonds and continued with the diamond jack, overtaking with dummy's king. Both defenders followed but the ace did not appear. Preparing to claim the contract, declarer led a third round of hearts from dummy. It was an embarrassing moment when East showed out. West scored two heart tricks and led a third round of clubs. There was no entry to dummy to take the spade finesse and the game went one down.

> ### TOP TIP
>
> There are many situations where the defenders can make declarer believe that a finesse has succeeded, thereby drawing him into a losing line of play. Suppose dummy holds A-J-9 in a side suit and you are sitting over the dummy with K-Q-10-x. When declarer finesses the nine, it costs little to win with a deceptive king or queen. Declarer may then hope that a subsequent finesse of the jack will succeed, perhaps wasting an entry or losing the chance to pursue some other line that would have succeeded.

'Too clever by far!' observed the North player. 'Use your entry to dummy to take the spade finesse and you make it easily.'

We can do without partners who make such comments. Even if West was a tricky customer, well capable of a false card, the

Principle of Restricted Choice made declarer's play in hearts a huge favourite over a simple spade finesse. His line of play could not be faulted.

Suppose you are defending a small slam and hold K-J-x in the trump suit. Is there any way you can deflect declarer from a successful safety play in trumps? 'Yes,' said East when the following deal arose:

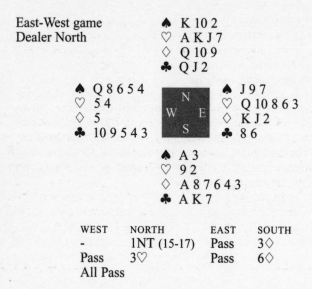

East-West game
Dealer North

♠ K 10 2
♡ A K J 7
◇ Q 10 9
♣ Q J 2

♠ Q 8 6 5 4
♡ 5 4
◇ 5
♣ 10 9 5 4 3

♠ J 9 7
♡ Q 10 8 6 3
◇ K J 2
♣ 8 6

♠ A 3
♡ 9 2
◇ A 8 7 6 4 3
♣ A K 7

WEST	NORTH	EAST	SOUTH
-	1NT (15-17)	Pass	3◇
Pass	3♡	Pass	6◇
All Pass			

South's 3◇ was a single-suited slam try and North's 3♡ was a cue-bid agreeing diamonds. West led the ♡5 and declarer won with dummy's ace. Suppose you had been sitting East. Would you expect to score two trump tricks or not?

East at the table did his best to ensure that he did score two trump tricks. At Trick 1 he followed with the queen of hearts, pretending that it was singleton. Any form of delicate play in the trump suit (running the queen, or leading low from the South hand) now seemed to be fraught with danger. West might win with the trump king and give his partner a heart ruff. Declarer duly hammered out ace and another trump, going one down.

East's false card was believable because West might well have led the five when holding 10-8-6-5-4-3. Suppose East had started with Q-10-9-8-6. It would be a waste of time playing the queen, because declarer would not believe a lead of the five from 10-9-8-6-5-3. Indeed, his suspicions would be aroused that you had a trump holding worth protecting.

Suppose East follows with a low heart and there is no reason to expect a ruff. What is the best play in trumps? Mathematically best is to lead low to the ten. If this loses to

the jack, you play the ace next. This is because any particular 2-2 break, such as K-2 opposite J-5, is slightly more likely than any particular 1-3 break, such as 2 opposite K-J-5. This ignores the human factor that many West players with a doubleton king may play the card, or at least consider doing so, when you lead towards dummy. In practice this is enough to induce you to run the queen on the second round.

On our next deal West drew declarer down a losing path by pretending that the trump suit lay in a particular way. See if you think that declarer should have made the contract anyway.

Love all
Dealer West

```
                    ♠ 9 7 5 4
                    ♡ A K 7 5 4
                    ◇ A 2
                    ♣ A 7
♠ Q J 3                         ♠ 6
♡ 3                 N           ♡ Q J 10 9 6
◇ K Q J 10 8    W       E       ◇ 9 6 4 3
♣ K Q 10 3          S           ♣ J 8 5
                    ♠ A K 10 8 2
                    ♡ 8 2
                    ◇ 7 5
                    ♣ 9 6 4 2
```

WEST	NORTH	EAST	SOUTH
1◇	1♡	Pass	1♠
Pass	4♠	All Pass	

Declarer won the ◇K lead with dummy's ace and continued with a trump to the ace. On this trick West dropped the queen! Seeing an easy route home, declarer crossed to dummy with the ♡A and led another trump, intending to cover East's card. If a trump finesse lost to an original Q-J doubleton, there would be two trumps left in dummy to deal with two of South's club losers.

A small flaw in this plan emerged when East showed out on the second trump. Declarer felt a tinge of sweat. Was he about to go down in a cold contract? Surely not, he thought. If the hearts split 4-2 he would be able to set up a long heart. He won the second round of trumps and led a second heart to the king, not overjoyed to see West show out. His next move was to ruff a heart. If West were to overruff, declarer would be back on track again — dummy's two small trumps could be used to ruff clubs.

No, West was not going to waste the effect of his earlier false card. He discarded a diamond instead of overruffing. Declarer led a club to the ace and ruffed another heart. Once again West refused to overruff, throwing a diamond. Declarer had no option now but to concede a club. When West won and drew a third round of trumps, the contract was defeated. Excellent defence, yes, but should declarer have made the contract anyway? What do you think?

The contract is easily made if declarer simply gives up a club at Trick 2. When he regains the lead he can draw two rounds of trumps and continue happily with his cross-ruff.

We move now to some deals where the defenders attempt to disguise their holding in a side suit. By far the most important technique available is the humble hold-up play, which is much underrated as a deceptive weapon.

> **TOP TIP**
>
> Suppose you are aiming for an eventual cross-ruff and have a trump holding of A-K-x-x(-x) opposite x-x-x-x. It is often right to prepare for the cross-ruff, by conceding losers in the suits you intend to ruff, before you cash the ace and king of trumps. If you play the top trumps first, you run the risk that the defenders will draw a third round of trumps when you surrender the lead.

Love all
Dealer South

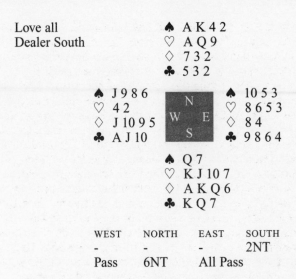

	♠ A K 4 2	
	♡ A Q 9	
	◇ 7 3 2	
	♣ 5 3 2	

♠ J 9 8 6		♠ 10 5 3
♡ 4 2		♡ 8 6 5 3
◇ J 10 9 5		◇ 8 4
♣ A J 10		♣ 9 8 6 4

	♠ Q 7	
	♡ K J 10 7	
	◇ A K Q 6	
	♣ K Q 7	

WEST	NORTH	EAST	SOUTH
-	-	-	2NT
Pass	6NT	All Pass	

Declarer won the ◇J lead with the ace and crossed to dummy with a heart. It was only Trick 3 but when he played a club to the king the key moment of the hand had been reached. What would most West players do? They would win with the ♣A and return the ♣J. Knowing that one trick in clubs was his ration, declarer would be down to two main possibilities — that the diamonds were 3-3, or that the same defender held the spade and diamond guards. He would cash his remaining winners in hearts and West would be squeezed, forced to throw either his spade or his diamond guard.

Since South's opening bid promised at least 20 points, West can see that he holds all the defence's honour cards. The risk of a squeeze is clear and he should attempt to deflect declarer from this path. Suppose he plays the ♣J under South's king at Trick 3. At double-dummy it is still possible for declarer to squeeze West (it will be a triple squeeze, in fact). However, he will surely conclude that his best chance is to find East with the ace of clubs. It will be a nasty moment for him when a club to the queen loses to West's ace and West finds yet another club to beat the contract!

The next deal comes from the high-stake rubber bridge table at TGR's Club in London. New Zealand's Lionel Wright was sitting in the West seat.

North-South game
Dealer South

```
                    ♠ A Q 10 4
                    ♡ A 4 2
                    ◇ Q 4 3
                    ♣ A K 2
  ♠ K 8 7                        ♠ J 9 6 2
  ♡ Q J 8 5         N            ♡ -
  ◇ J 10 9 6    W       E        ◇ 8 2
  ♣ 8 6             S            ♣ Q J 10 9 7 5 3
                    ♠ 5 3
                    ♡ K 10 9 7 6 3
                    ◇ A K 7 5
                    ♣ 4
```

WEST	NORTH	EAST	SOUTH
-	-	-	1♡
Pass	1♠	Pass	2♡
Pass	3♣	Pass	3◇
Pass	6♡	All Pass	

Wright led the ◇J against the heart slam and declarer won in his hand, continuing with a trump to the ace. Plans to claim the contract had to be abandoned when East showed out. The only chance now was to strip West of his side-suit cards and then end-play him in the trump suit. Realising that West would need to hold at least three diamonds, declarer played on that suit next. East showed out on the third round and declarer continued by playing two top clubs, discarding a spade. Declarer cashed the ♠A to leave these cards out:

```
                    ♠ Q 10 4
                    ♡ 4 2
                    ◇ -
                    ♣ 2
  ♠ K 8                          ♠ J 9 6
  ♡ Q J 8           N            ♡ -
  ◇ 10          W       E        ◇ -
  ♣ -               S            ♣ Q J 10
                    ♠ -
                    ♡ K 10 9 7 6
                    ◇ 7
                    ♣ -
```

When declarer ruffed a spade in his hand, Wright followed deceptively with the king. He could see that the established ♠Q would be of no use to declarer. It was more important to mislead him as to the shape of the West hand. Declarer ruffed his last diamond in dummy and, concluding that West had no more spades, attempted to reach his hand with a club ruff. Unlucky! Wright overruffed and was able to exit safely with a spade. He scored a second trump trick a second or two later and the slam was one down.

What can declarer do to counter such deceptions? It's not usually much use looking closely at the cards played by the key defender (West here). He will be alive to what is going on and, as we saw, can take whatever steps occur to him to disguise his shape. You will generally find it more useful to look at the other defender's cards. Suppose the defenders are playing distributional discards, where a high card shows an even number of cards in the suit. Unaware that deception may be critical in some distant end position, East may well throw an honest ♣3 to show an odd number

---

TOP TIP

In general, be willing to believe the distributional signals made by the defenders. In particular, you can usually rely on the signals made by the partner of the defender who is in some difficulty with his discards.

---

of clubs. Any deceptive effort West may make after that will be in vain.

7
Reading the Cards

What is the greatest aid to reading the defenders' cards? It is no great mystery — the answer is counting. Perhaps you play bridge for enjoyment and think that counting the hand is too much like hard work. It is a perfectly reasonable view to take but don't expect to be a regular winner at the table!

We will start with a straightforward example of counting, a deal played many years ago at Stefan's Bridge Circle. The declarer was Leo Baron, inventor of what might be called the first scientific bidding system.

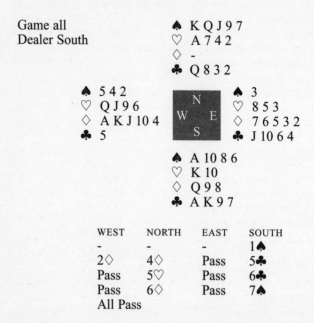

Game all
Dealer South

```
              ♠ K Q J 9 7
              ♡ A 7 4 2
              ◇ -
              ♣ Q 8 3 2
♠ 5 4 2                        ♠ 3
♡ Q J 9 6          N          ♡ 8 5 3
◇ A K J 10 4   W     E        ◇ 7 6 5 3 2
♣ 5                S          ♣ J 10 6 4
              ♠ A 10 8 6
              ♡ K 10
              ◇ Q 9 8
              ♣ A K 9 7
```

WEST	NORTH	EAST	SOUTH
-	-	-	1♠
2◇	4◇	Pass	5♣
Pass	5♡	Pass	6♣
Pass	6◇	Pass	7♠
All Pass			

Baron ruffed the diamond lead in dummy and played the king and ace of hearts. A heart ruff in his hand was followed by a trump to dummy and a second heart ruff with the ace. This was the position after trumps had been drawn:

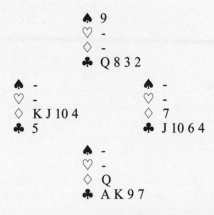

♠ 9
♡ -
◇ -
♣ Q 8 3 2

♠ -   ♠ -
♡ -   ♡ -
◇ K J 10 4   ◇ 7
♣ 5   ♣ J 10 6 4

♠ -
♡ -
◇ Q
♣ A K 9 7

Baron played the dummy's queen of clubs and continued with a low club, finessing the nine. He was then able to claim the remainder. It would have done East no good to split his club honours, of course, because declarer could win and return to dummy with a diamond ruff to pick up the remainder of the club suit.

How did declarer know the lie of the club suit? Because he had counted the hand. West had shown up with three trumps, four hearts and one club. His overcall had indicated at least five diamonds, so there was no room left for another club. Not a very difficult contract but how many players at your local club would make it? No more than a quarter of them, you can be sure. That's because the major-

> **TOP TIP**
>
> If you know how the defenders' cards break in a key suit, it is easier to play the suit to good effect. Suppose you hold ♣A-J-x-x in dummy and ♣K-10-x-x in your hand. If East holds three clubs to West's two, you should finesse East for the missing queen. To determine the defenders' club lengths you should play on the other suits to obtain a complete count of the hand.

ity of bridge players cannot be bothered to count the hand. Become one of the few… and you will leap ahead of them!

On the next deal you have a key decision to make in the club suit. After calculating which lies of the club suit will permit the contract to be made, you must decide which of them is more likely.

Love all
Dealer East

```
              ♠ J 10 9 5
              ♡ K 9
              ◇ 7 6
              ♣ K 8 6 4 3
♠ 8 4                        ♠ 3 2
♡ Q 8 7        N             ♡ A J 6 5
◇ Q J 10 5 4   W   E         ◇ K 9 8 3 2
♣ A 9 2            S         ♣ Q 7
              ♠ A K Q 7 6
              ♡ 10 4 3 2
              ◇ A
              ♣ J 10 5
```

WEST	NORTH	EAST	SOUTH
-	-	Pass	1♠
Pass	2♠	Pass	3♡
Pass	4♠	All Pass	

West leads the ◇Q and you win with the bare ace. You draw trumps and find that they break 2-2. How will you continue?

All will be easy if West holds the ♡A, so you should mentally place this card with East. You must now calculate how to tackle the club suit. Provided you first ruff dummy's remaining diamond, you can sometimes end-play East in clubs. On the lie of the cards shown in the diagram, for example, you can play a club to the king. East will have to win the second round with the bare queen and will be end-played. He will have to concede a ruff-and-discard (allowing you to dispose of your remaining club loser) or lead a heart up to dummy's king.

How good is it to lead the ♣J instead? You will win by force when East holds ♣A-9-7, ♣A-7-2, ♣9-7, or ♣9. You may also be able to guess correctly on the second round when East started with ♣A-9 or ♣A-9-2. Other things being equal, it

TOP TIP

When you need a particular defender to hold a missing king or ace, mentally place that card with him. A secondary assumption may follow from this. For example, suppose East opened a 12-14 point 1NT and has already shown up with ten points in the majors. If you are forced to assume that he holds the ♣A, this brings his point-count to 14. You should finesse West for a missing ◇Q.

looks better to run the jack on the first round. However, East is known from the opening lead to hold the ◇K. You are placing him also with the ♡A. Give him the ♣A as well and he might have had enough to open the bidding (he may hold one of the heart honours too). This factor is enough to swing you towards the winning play. You should eliminate the diamonds and play a club to dummy's king.

The next deal comes from the Young Chelsea Club 24-hour marathon. Martin was North and the time was three in the morning! To make the contract his partner had to guess which major suit might break badly. The only clue to guide him was that West had opened the bidding. Would you have drawn the right conclusion?

North-South game
Dealer West

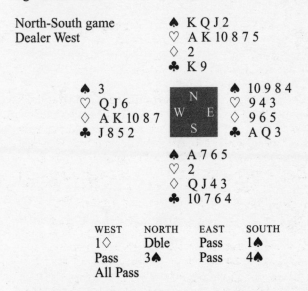

```
                  ♠ K Q J 2
                  ♡ A K 10 8 7 5
                  ◇ 2
                  ♣ K 9

   ♠ 3                        ♠ 10 9 8 4
   ♡ Q J 6            N       ♡ 9 4 3
   ◇ A K 10 8 7   W       E   ◇ 9 6 5
   ♣ J 8 5 2           S       ♣ A Q 3

                  ♠ A 7 6 5
                  ♡ 2
                  ◇ Q J 4 3
                  ♣ 10 7 6 4
```

WEST	NORTH	EAST	SOUTH
1◇	Dble	Pass	1♠
Pass	3♠	Pass	4♠
All Pass			

West led the ◇A and switched to the ♣2. Dummy's king lost to the ace and East cashed the queen of clubs. The ◇9 return was covered by the queen and king, ruffed in the dummy. How would you continue the play from this point?

At the table declarer decided to cater for a 4-2 heart break. He cashed the ace of hearts, ruffed a heart low and returned to dummy with a trump. A second heart ruff was taken with the ace, but the contract fell apart when West showed out on the second round of trumps.

Everything depended on reading the shape of the West hand. By the time East had shown up with the queen and ace of clubs, it was apparent that West had opened on at most eleven points. He was therefore likely to have a bit of distribution, probably including a singleton. Should you play West for 1-3-5-4 or 3-1-5-4 shape? The latter possibility is remote because he would then hold at most ten points including a singleton ♡Q. More important, you cannot even make the contract if West has a singleton heart!

There is every reason, then, to place West with a singleton spade. In that case you will need hearts to divide 3-3. You should cash the ace and king of hearts and ruff a heart low. When your reading of the cards proves to have been gilt-edged, you cross to dummy with a trump and lead good hearts through East. If he ruffs at any stage you will overruff with the ace and return to dummy's remaining trump honours, drawing trumps and claiming the balance. Game made!

Martin played the next hand himself, in a Summer Congress Swiss Pairs at Brighton. Take the South cards yourself and see if you can find a way to give the defenders a problem.

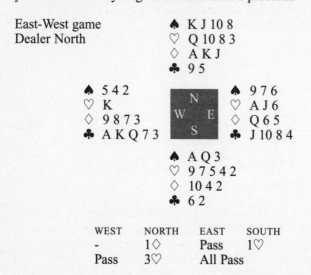

East-West game
Dealer North

	♠ K J 10 8
	♡ Q 10 8 3
	◇ A K J
	♣ 9 5

♠ 5 4 2		♠ 9 7 6
♡ K		♡ A J 6
◇ 9 8 7 3		◇ Q 6 5
♣ A K Q 7 3		♣ J 10 8 4

	♠ A Q 3
	♡ 9 7 5 4 2
	◇ 10 4 2
	♣ 6 2

WEST	NORTH	EAST	SOUTH
-	1◇	Pass	1♡
Pass	3♡	All Pass	

You think North's raise to 3♡ was an overbid? We agree with you! West played the ace and king of clubs (East playing a discouraging four and then the eight) and switched to the ◇9. Martin rose with dummy's ace and had to decide how to play the trump suit. What would you have done?

The normal play with this holding is to lead a low card from the South hand, finessing the ten. You will then lose only two tricks when East holds a singleton ace or king. Since West had not overcalled, despite holding an excellent club suit, it was hardly possible for him to hold A-J-6 or K-J-6 of hearts. Martin preferred to lead the queen of hearts from the dummy! This would succeed, technically, if West held a singleton jack. There was also a chance that East would go wrong when West held a singleton ace or king.

You will have guessed by now what happened. Placing declarer with the trump king, East captured dummy's queen with the ace. West shook his head as he contributed the king to this trick and the contract was made, declarer's potential diamond loser going on dummy's spade suit. East's play of the trump ace does not stand up to close scrutiny but it is the sort of error that many players would make, also from K-J-x. Give the defenders a chance to go wrong and, more often than you think, they will take it.

We will look next at some contracts that apparently depend on a 50-50 guess. In each case a skilled practitioner can bend the odds in his favour. The original declarer was somewhat less than skilled when this deal arose at rubber bridge:

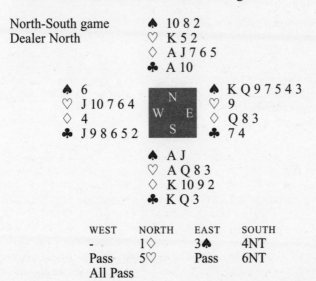

North-South game   ♠ 10 8 2
Dealer North   ♡ K 5 2
                 ◇ A J 7 6 5
                 ♣ A 10

♠ 6   ♠ K Q 9 7 5 4 3
♡ J 10 7 6 4   ♡ 9
◇ 4   ◇ Q 8 3
♣ J 9 8 6 5 2   ♣ 7 4

                 ♠ A J
                 ♡ A Q 8 3
                 ◇ K 10 9 2
                 ♣ K Q 3

WEST	NORTH	EAST	SOUTH
-	1◇	3♠	4NT
Pass	5♡	Pass	6NT
All Pass			

West led his singleton spade and declarer captured East's queen with the ace. It seemed that success in the small slam would hinge on guessing who held the ◇Q. The opening lead was doubtless a singleton but finessing diamonds into the safe hand would not guarantee the contract. A losing diamond finesse would leave declarer with only eleven tricks and he would then need an unlikely 3-3 heart break (or an even more unlikely major-suit squeeze against East). How would you have played the slam?

Reasoning that West held one spade to his partner's seven and was therefore a clear favourite to hold the diamond queen, declarer cashed the king of diamonds and led another diamond. One down!

The best idea on deals of this sort is a little detective work. Suppose you return the jack of spades at Trick 2. This will confirm that East did indeed start with seven cards in the suit. You win his return and cash three rounds of both hearts and clubs. As it happens, East shows up with one heart and two clubs, marking his shape as 7-1-3-2.

The guess in diamonds has become a certainty. Contrary to the initial odds, it is East who holds three diamonds to his partner's one. You cash the ace of diamonds and finesse the diamond ten with complete confidence. Only if East follows to three clubs and one heart will there be any doubt. He might then be 7-1-2-3 or 7-1-1-4. However, West may have given the game away when you played your club winners. Many defenders signal their count as a matter of course — not that it makes much sense on a slam deal like this.

You are perhaps familiar with this position:

◇ K 10 7 3

◇ J 9 6 4   ◇ 2

◇ A Q 8 5

You keep all options open by cashing the ace first. It is well known that West should drop the nine on the first round. This creates a two-way guess where one did not exist previously. So, what should you do when you cash the ace and the nine comes from your left-hand opponent? If he is a good player, well capable of the false card, you should assume that he holds J-9-x-x and cash the queen next. This is especially the case if diamonds are a side suit and West might have led a singleton nine initially. If the suit is trumps and West is a weak player, incapable of a clever card in your judgement, it is best to assume that the nine is a singleton.

Let's look at a whole deal involving such a jack guess.

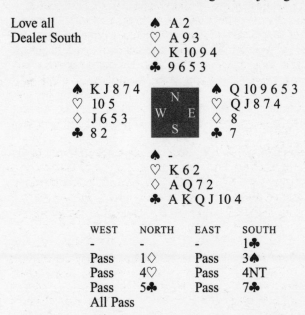

Love all
Dealer South

♠ A 2
♡ A 9 3
◇ K 10 9 4
♣ 9 6 5 3

♠ K J 8 7 4
♡ 10 5
◇ J 6 5 3
♣ 8 2

♠ Q 10 9 6 5 3
♡ Q J 8 7 4
◇ 8
♣ 7

♠ -
♡ K 6 2
◇ A Q 7 2
♣ A K Q J 10 4

WEST	NORTH	EAST	SOUTH
-	-	-	1♣
Pass	1◇	Pass	3♠
Pass	4♡	Pass	4NT
Pass	5♣	Pass	7♣
All Pass			

South temporarily agreed diamonds as trumps with his splinter-bid of 3♠. The subsequent 4NT was Roman Key-card Blackwood, the response showing two aces and the diamond king. West led a trump and declarer drew trumps in two rounds. The heart loser could be discarded on the ace of spades, so all depended on picking up the diamond suit. When declarer cashed the ace of diamonds, the six appeared from West and the eight from East. How would you have continued?

West may be attempting to mislead you from ◇J-6-5-3 and so may East, from ◇J-8-5-3. If you knew for sure that a defender with four diamonds to the jack would always play his highest spot-card, then the odds would be 3-to-1 that the defender playing the ◇8 held the length. (There are three J-8-x-x combinations and only one J-6-x-x.) How should you proceed?

On this deal, and on many others like it, you should play on the other suits before making your critical guess. By doing so, you hope to build up a picture of the defenders' distribution. Cash the king and ace of hearts and throw your third heart on the ace of spades. When you ruff dummy's last heart West shows out! If West's shape outside spades were 2-1-2 he would hold an eight-card spade suit. This is extremely unlikely, particularly as he failed to bid over your 1♣. You should therefore play West for the diamond length — a move that pays off on this occasion.

On the next deal the defenders force declarer to a king-jack guess early in the play, before he has the chance to seek any further information. Would you have guessed right?

East-West game
Dealer West

♠ 5 4
♡ 10 9 6 3 2
◇ J 7
♣ A 10 9 3

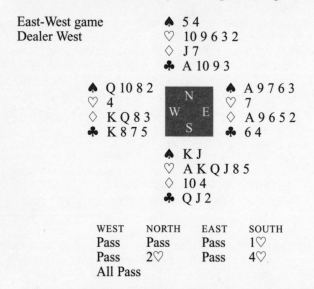

♠ Q 10 8 2
♡ 4
◇ K Q 8 3
♣ K 8 7 5

♠ A 9 7 6 3
♡ 7
◇ A 9 6 5 2
♣ 6 4

♠ K J
♡ A K Q J 8 5
◇ 10 4
♣ Q J 2

WEST	NORTH	EAST	SOUTH
Pass	Pass	Pass	1♡
Pass	2♡	Pass	4♡
All Pass			

West leads the ◇K, winning the first trick, and continues with the queen of diamonds. If East allows the queen to win, ten tricks will easily be made. West cannot attack spades from his side and declarer will eventually discard a spade on the fourth round of clubs. East was a sound performer, however, and overtook with the ace of diamonds on the second round. (Overtaking on the first round would have been even better, in case declarer held only one diamond.) At Trick 3 East returned a low spade. Suppose you had been South. What thoughts would have gone through your head as you decided which spade honour to play?

The original declarer subscribed to the theory that two outstanding aces were likely to be split between the defenders. Since East had already shown up with the diamond ace he placed the spade ace with West. He inserted the jack of spades and lost two spade tricks to go one down.

The deal is an illustration of what is known as 'secondary assumption'. You cannot make the contract unless West holds the ♣K and should therefore assume that he holds this card. Since that will give him eight points in the minors, and he neither opened the bidding nor entered with a second-round double, he cannot hold the spade ace too. You should play East for the spade ace and rise with the spade king. The club king is indeed onside and you make the game.

Our next deal comes from a clash of giants in the Macallan International Pairs, played in London. Brazilian maestro, Marcelo Branco, is the declarer.

Game all
Dealer South

♠ A 10
♡ Q J 8
♢ 10 8 7 3
♣ Q 9 3 2

♠ 6 5 4 3 2　　　♠ -
♡ K 10 7 6　　　♡ A 9 5 4
♢ Q 4　　　　　♢ K 9 5
♣ 6 5　　　　　♣ K J 10 8 7 4

♠ K Q J 9 8 7
♡ 3 2
♢ A J 6 2
♣ A

WEST	NORTH	EAST	SOUTH
Zia	Chagas	Rosenberg	Branco
-	-	-	1♠
Pass	1NT	2♣	2♢
Pass	2NT	Pass	3♠
Pass	4♠	All Pass	

Zia led the ♣6 and Branco won with the bare ace. With two certain heart losers, all would depend on picking up the diamond suit for just one loser. Branco decided to gather some more information about the distribution before making the key decision. At Trick 2 he led a low heart from his hand. Zia must have been distracted by the bevy of beautiful females at his elbow. If he rises with the heart king and plays another club, attacking declarer's trump length, the contract is doomed. He played low, however, and Rosenberg won with the ace of hearts. A heart to West's king was followed by a second club, ruffed by declarer.

Branco crossed to dummy with the ace of trumps, discovering the hostile break in the suit. These cards remained:

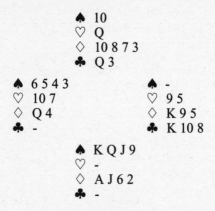

Branco now needed to read the lie of the diamond suit. If East held both the missing diamond honours, the contract would fail anyway because East would gain the lead to play the ♣K. A finesse of the diamond jack would pick up a doubleton diamond honour with East. This was barely a possible holding, though, because East would have bid differently with 0-5-2-6 shape. The only remaining holding that he could pick up was K-9-x or Q-9-x. Branco called for the ◇3 from dummy. Rosenberg followed with the five and declarer inserted the six!

There was no defence at this point. Zia took the trick with the diamond queen and returned a trump. Branco won with dummy's ♠10, played a diamond to the jack and drew trumps. He could then claim the contract. Suppose instead that Zia allows declarer's ◇6 to win. Declarer will then cash the diamond ace and cross to dummy's ♠10 to discard his penultimate diamond on the heart queen.

Does anything else strike you about the way the play went?

Look back to the eight-card end position. When Branco led the ◇3 from dummy, Rosenberg could have beaten the contract by inserting the nine! West wins declarer's jack with the queen and plays a trump to the dummy. Dummy's diamond spot-card is allowed to win the next trick and declarer cannot leave the dummy without allowing West a ruff or a trump promotion. Yes, Branco should have led the ten, eight or seven on the first round of diamonds.

> **TOP TIP**
>
> Suppose you hold 10-8-7-2 in dummy and A-Q-6-3 in your hand. You lead to the queen on the first round. If this loses, you hope to drop the jack on the next round. If you are short of entries to your hand, it may be beneficial to lead the 8 for the initial finesse of the queen. If this loses and the ace (on which you drop the 7) fails to drop the jack, you can then lead to dummy's 10 on the third round. This will leave you with a fourth-round entry to the South hand.

Reading the cards is usually critical when you are playing for a trump end-play. To reduce your left-hand opponent to Q-10-9 of trumps, before throwing him in from your own K-J-7, you will have to extract all of his side-suit cards. If you make one false step, trying to cash the wrong card, the defender will ruff and exit safely. Declarer performed some imaginative detective work on this deal.

Love all
Dealer South

```
              ♠ 9 8 6 5 2
              ♡ 10 9 7
              ◇ Q
              ♣ K 10 8 4
  ♠ Q 10 7 4            ♠ -
  ♡ A 3          N       ♡ 8 6 5 4
  ◇ K 10 6    W   E      ◇ 9 8 7 5 4 3
  ♣ A J 6 2      S       ♣ 9 7 5
              ♠ A K J 3
              ♡ K Q J 2
              ◇ A J 2
              ♣ Q 3
```

WEST	NORTH	EAST	SOUTH
-	-	-	2NT
Pass	3♡	Pass	3♠
Pass	3NT	Pass	4♠
All Pass			

South ended in 4♠ after a transfer auction. West resisted the temptation to double and decided to lead one of his aces before the rats could get at them. He led the ♡A and, on seeing that the dummy had only low trumps, lost no time in cashing his ♣A too. Declarer won the heart continuation and played the ace of trumps, discovering that West had two apparent trump winners.

To make the game now, declarer needed to reduce the West hand to his three remaining trumps. What distributions of the West hand would permit this? If West's shape was 4-4-3-2, it would be easy enough to ruff two diamonds and to cash three hearts and one club. If West was 4-3-3-3, declarer would have to take only two more heart winners and two clubs. Finally, if West's shape was 4-2-3-4, declarer would need to cash only one more heart winner and two clubs, ruffing two diamonds in the dummy and one club in his hand. How would you attempt to read the cards?

Declarer made a clever move. After discovering the bad trump break, he cashed the ace of diamonds and ruffed a diamond. He then led the ♣10 from the dummy. East followed low and declarer won with the bare queen. When West followed with the two, it was a near certainty that he held at least one more club. Otherwise East would hold the jack and nine of clubs and would surely have covered dummy's ♣10.

Declarer returned to dummy with a second diamond ruff and cashed the king of clubs, discarding a heart from his hand. The fall of East's ♣9 marked West with the missing ♣J. Declarer therefore ruffed a club, successfully removing West's last plain card. It remained only to exit with a small trump and the game was made.

Do you see how West might have made life a little more difficult for declarer? After cashing his two aces, he should have exited with the ♣J, feigning shortage in the suit. It would then have been no easy task for declarer to divine how the cards lay.

8

The Squeeze
Without the Count

Most books on squeezes over-emphasise the need to rectify the count (to lose at an early stage those tricks that you can afford to lose). While this procedure is often necessary, many squeezes survive without it.

Let's start with a typical 'squeeze without the count', a squeeze where the count has not been rectified. Declarer will lose a trick after the squeeze has taken effect.

North-South game
Dealer South

```
            ♠ K 9 4
            ♡ J 3 2
            ◇ A Q 7
            ♣ A Q J 7

♠ Q J 10 6 3              ♠ 8 5
♡ K Q 7          N        ♡ 10 9 8 6 4
◇ 10 6 3      W     E     ◇ 9 8 4 2
♣ 3 2            S        ♣ 9 6

            ♠ A 7 2
            ♡ A 5
            ◇ K J 5
            ♣ K 10 8 5 4
```

WEST	NORTH	EAST	SOUTH
-	-	-	1♣
1♠	Dble	Pass	1NT (15-17)
Pass	6NT	All Pass	

How would you play the no-trump slam when West leads the queen of spades?

There are eleven top tricks and the only real chance of a twelfth is to squeeze West in the majors. Normally, when attempting such a squeeze, you would duck an early trick to tighten the end position. You cannot duck a heart here because West would return a spade, leaving you with no entry to dummy in the end-game. Instead you should win the spade lead with the ace and run your minor-suit winners straight away. This end position results:

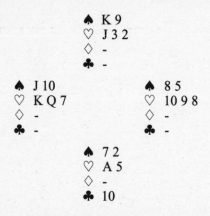

♠ K 9
♡ J 3 2
◇ -
♣ -

♠ J 10   ♠ 8 5
♡ K Q 7   ♡ 10 9 8
◇ -   ◇ -
♣ -   ♣ -

♠ 7 2
♡ A 5
◇ -
♣ 10

West has no good discard on the ♣10. If he throws a spade, you will discard a heart from dummy and dummy's ♠K-9 will score two tricks. If West throws a heart instead, you will discard the ♠9 from dummy and play ace and another heart to set up dummy's ♡J. It's the sort of deal where someone who knew almost nothing about squeezes might stumble onto the winning line.

On many squeezes without the count you need to read the cards accurately, to judge in which suit the key defender has weakened his guard. It was no problem on the last deal because West could be placed with the ♠J-10 and neither of these cards had appeared when you had to make your last discard from dummy.

That is one form of the squeeze without the count, then. West was forced to reduce his double guard on hearts and you could then give up a heart trick to set up a winner in the suit. The other common form ends with a throw-in. A defender is put on lead and has to lead into a tenace. Before the throw-in can take place he has to be squeezed out of his safe exit cards. That's what happened on this deal, played by Phil Karani in the Teams at Casablanca.

Love all
Dealer South

♠ K 7 3 2
♥ J 5 4
♦ K 9 4 2
♣ A 2

♠ J 10 5   ♠ Q 9 8 6
♥ 10 9 8   ♥ K 7 6 3
♦ 6 5   ♦ 3
♣ K J 9 8 5   ♣ Q 10 6 3

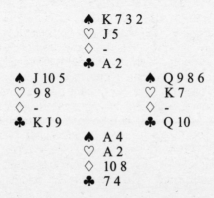

♠ A 4
♥ A Q 2
♦ A Q J 10 8 7
♣ 7 4

WEST	NORTH	EAST	SOUTH
	Hoffman		Karani
-	-	-	1♦
Pass	1♠	Pass	3♦
Pass	4♣	Pass	4♥
Pass	6♦	All Pass	

Declarer won the heart lead with the queen. One small chance
was that East had started with a doubleton ♥K. A more likely
possibility was that East had started with four or more spades
and could be thrown in on the fourth round to lead away from the
♥K. Since East could not be allowed a safe exit in clubs, his
clubs would have to be squeezed out of him before the throw-in
took place.

Karani ran four rounds of trumps, reaching this position:

♠ K 7 3 2
♥ J 5
♦ -
♣ A 2

♠ J 10 5   ♠ Q 9 8 6
♥ 9 8   ♥ K 7
♦ -   ♦ -
♣ K J 9   ♣ Q 10

♠ A 4
♥ A 2
♦ 10 8
♣ 7 4

Declarer played his penultimate trump, throwing a club from dummy. East could not afford a major-suit discard, so had to throw one of his clubs. In other words he was squeezed out of his safe exit card. Some writers, particularly in America, do not refer to this play as a squeeze. They call it the strip-and-endplay, whereas in Europe it is known as a strip squeeze. You can see that East is squeezed out of an important card, his spare club.

Karani continued with the ace and king of spades, followed by a spade ruff. A club to dummy's ace then allowed him to throw East on lead with dummy's last spade. The enforced heart return was run to dummy's jack and the slam was made.

Did anything else occur to you about that deal? A club lead would have beaten the slam! Declarer needed the ♣A as a late entry to dummy, to reach the throw-in card.

On the next deal West's bidding makes the defenders' distribution clear.

North-South game
Dealer South

♠ 3 2
♡ 6 5 4 2
◇ 3
♣ K Q 8 7 6 4

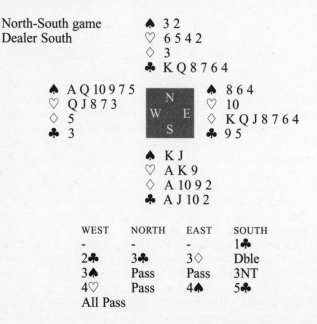

♠ A Q 10 9 7 5
♡ Q J 8 7 3
◇ 5
♣ 3

♠ 8 6 4
♡ 10
◇ K Q J 8 7 6 4
♣ 9 5

♠ K J
♡ A K 9
◇ A 10 9 2
♣ A J 10 2

WEST	NORTH	EAST	SOUTH
-	-	-	1♣
2♣	3♣	3◇	Dble
3♠	Pass	Pass	3NT
4♡	Pass	4♠	5♣
All Pass			

West's 2♣ was the popular Michaels cue-bid, showing length in both majors. His subsequent removal of 3◇ doubled to 3♠ suggested that he was 6-5 in the majors. How would you play the club game when West leads the ◇5?

Had there been no adverse bidding, you would probably try to duck a heart into the safe West hand, hoping for a 3-3 heart break, with the spade guess in reserve. Here declarer had a clear picture of West's shape in the majors and it was clear from the outset that he could be caught in a squeeze without the count.

Declarer won the diamond lead and ruffed a diamond. Returning to his hand with the ♣10, he ruffed another

> ## TOP TIP
>
> Suppose an opponent overcalls with a two-suited bid, such as the Unusual No-trump or a Michaels cue-bid, and you end up playing the hand. It is usually very easy to obtain a complete count on the hand. For example, West bids 2NT and eventually leads the ♡6 against your contract of 4♠. It is already a fair bet that his shape is 2-1-5-5. If instead he leads one of the minors, he will probably be 1-2-5-5 with a singleton trump.

diamond. A trump to the jack permitted a third diamond ruff. A trump to the ace left this position:

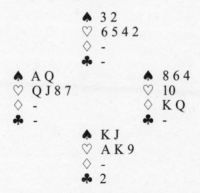

```
              ♠ 3 2
              ♡ 6 5 4 2
              ◇ -
              ♣ -
  ♠ A Q                    ♠ 8 6 4
  ♡ Q J 8 7                ♡ 10
  ◇ -                      ◇ K Q
  ♣ -                      ♣ -
              ♠ K J
              ♡ A K 9
              ◇ -
              ♣ 2
```

When declarer led his last trump West was forced to weaken one of his major-suit holdings. Hoping for the best, he discarded a heart. Declarer then played ace, king and another heart, throwing West on lead. After cashing the ace of spades, West had to surrender the last trick to South's spade king. As you see, the count was nowhere near rectified; declarer lost two tricks after the squeeze had taken place. West could hardly be faulted for entering the auction but such two-suited bids make the opponents' task very easy, should they end up playing the hand.

The next deal arose when Martin was partnering Zia Mahmood in the teams championship at Crans sur Sierre. If you think that the North-South cards were overbid somewhat, remember that Zia's reputation would be tarnished if he ever missed a 40% slam.

Game all
Dealer South

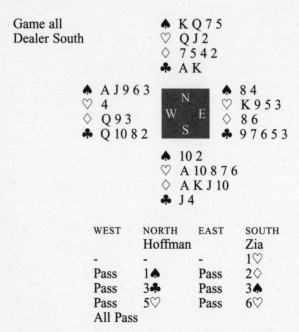

```
                    ♠ K Q 7 5
                    ♡ Q J 2
                    ◇ 7 5 4 2
                    ♣ A K
  ♠ A J 9 6 3                      ♠ 8 4
  ♡ 4              N               ♡ K 9 5 3
  ◇ Q 9 3      W       E           ◇ 8 6
  ♣ Q 10 8 2       S               ♣ 9 7 6 5 3
                    ♠ 10 2
                    ♡ A 10 8 7 6
                    ◇ A K J 10
                    ♣ J 4
```

WEST	NORTH	EAST	SOUTH
	Hoffman		Zia
-	-	-	1♡
Pass	1♠	Pass	2◇
Pass	3♣	Pass	3♠
Pass	5♡	Pass	6♡
All Pass			

West led a fourth-best ♣2, won in the dummy. The queen of trumps was run successfully and the jack of trumps was covered by the king and ace, West discarding a spade. A spade to the king won the next trick and Zia took the marked finesse of the trump eight, proceeding to draw East's last trump. West, meanwhile, threw one spade and two clubs. What next?

If declarer were to lead another spade towards the dummy at this stage, West would rise with the ace (to avoid a later throw-in). Dummy's ♠Q would provide an eleventh trick but there would be no way to score a twelfth. To make the slam declarer needed five tricks from spades and diamonds, not four. Zia paused for a few more seconds.

West had started with four clubs, if his opening lead was to be believed, and only one trump. Since East had started with nine cards to West's five in these suits, the omens were not good for the diamond finesse. Zia turned his mind towards a strip squeeze on West. He crossed to dummy's ♣K, removing West's last card in that suit and returned to the diamond ace. These cards remained:

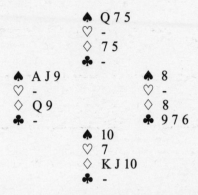

When Zia led this last trump, West had to retain both of his diamonds. He discarded the ♠9 and Zia then led a spade. West won with the ace and had to surrender the last two tricks either to dummy or declarer. He chose to exit in diamonds, in case his partner held the ◇J, and Zia claimed the remainder.

It would have done West no good to play the jack of spades instead, won by dummy's queen. He would then have been thrown in with a spade to lead into South's ◇Q-10.

Most squeezes where you have rectified the count do not require accurate card reading. As you play the squeeze-card you say to yourself: 'either they will throw the king of spades, establishing the queen, or I will have to hope that the diamonds are all good.' The same cannot be said about the squeeze without the count, unfortunately. You have to lose the lead after the squeeze has taken place and will therefore need to know what cards the key defender has kept.

On the next deal West has indicated a two-suiter in the auction and you plan to ruff one these suits good. You will need to read his shape, near the end of the play, in order to decide which suit you can establish.

Game all
Dealer South

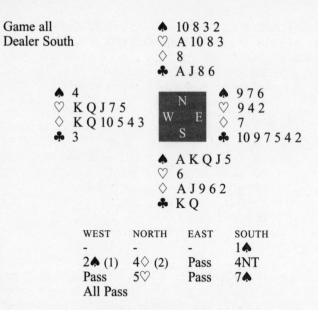

♠ 10 8 3 2
♡ A 10 8 3
◇ 8
♣ A J 8 6

♠ 4
♡ K Q J 7 5
◇ K Q 10 5 4 3
♣ 3

♠ 9 7 6
♡ 9 4 2
◇ 7
♣ 10 9 7 5 4 2

♠ A K Q J 5
♡ 6
◇ A J 9 6 2
♣ K Q

WEST	NORTH	EAST	SOUTH
-	-	-	1♠
2♠ (1)	4◇ (2)	Pass	4NT
Pass	5♡	Pass	7♠
All Pass			

(1) Michaels cue-bid, showing hearts and
one of the minors.
(2) Splinter bid, game raise with at most
one diamond.

West leads the ♡K against your grand slam and you win with
the ace. How should you aim for thirteen tricks?

Since you have a combined holding of six cards in both
diamonds and clubs, there is no early indication as to which
minor suit West holds. The Michaels overcall was vulnerable,
however, so his second suit is likely to contain an honour or two,
in which case it must be diamonds. Suppose you play ace of
diamonds, diamond ruff, king of clubs, diamond ruff high. You
will not be able to reach the
blocked club winners even if
trumps are 2-2 (in that case
West would be 2-5-5-1 and
would ruff the second club.)
Instead you should aim for one
diamond ruff, followed by a
red-suit squeeze on West.

At Trick 2 it is essential to

TOP TIP

It is a familiar process to ruff
high to prevent an overruff. The
same technique can be used in order
to preserve lower trumps for the
purpose of crossing to the other
hand.

ruff a heart with a high trump. You then draw two rounds of trumps in the South hand, West showing out on the second round. After unblocking the king and queen of clubs, you cross to dummy's ten of trumps and play dummy's top clubs. This will be the position when you lead the last club winner:

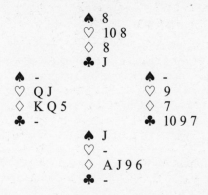

You discard a diamond on the ♣J and let's suppose that West throws the ♡J. What cards does he still have? Has he kept ♡Q-9 ◇ K-Q, in which case you must ruff a diamond good. Or does he have ♡Q ◇K-Q-5, in which case you must ruff a heart good?

You will rarely have a 50-50 guess in such a situation. First, look at the bidding. A hand with 1-5-6-1 shape is an obvious candidate for a Michaels overcall. With 1-6-5-1 and the hearts headed by the K-Q-J, many players would prefer to overcall in hearts. Secondly, did you note which spot-card East played to the first trick? He had no reason to deceive his partner and will almost certainly have played a true count card — here the ♡2, to indicate his three-card holding. These two pieces of evidence are enough to guide you. You ruff a heart and claim the contract when both defenders follow suit.

9
Reading Declarer's Mind

You cannot possibly defend well unless you know what declarer is trying to do. In this chapter we will look at several deals where a defender can counter declarer's plan, provided he realises in good time what it is!

This is a relatively simple deal where many defenders would go wrong:

East-West game
Dealer South

```
                    ♠ J 10 8 2
                    ♡ Q J 5
                    ◇ Q 8 4 2
                    ♣ 5 4
    ♠ 4                            ♠ 7 3
    ♡ A 9 7 6          N           ♡ K 10 4 2
    ◇ J 10 6 5      W     E        ◇ K 9 7
    ♣ 10 9 8 2         S           ♣ A J 7 6
                    ♠ A K Q 9 6 5
                    ♡ 8 3
                    ◇ A 3
                    ♣ K Q 3
```

WEST	NORTH	EAST	SOUTH
-	-	-	1♠
Pass	2♠	Pass	4♠
All Pass			

Sitting West, you lead the ♣10 to East's ace. Declarer wins the club return with the king and surprises you somewhat by leading a low heart at Trick 3. How will you defend?

Looking at the heart situation in isolation, it would often be right for you to play low on the first round. If declarer holds four hearts to the king, for example, rising with the ace would give him an undeserved third heart trick. Here, however, you know that a third heart trick would be valueless to declarer. If he does hold four hearts he can ruff the fourth round in dummy anyway. A more likely situation is that he holds only two hearts and is hoping to establish a discard on dummy's heart holding.

Suppose you play low on the first round of hearts. Your partner will win with the king but will not be able to attack diamonds successfully from his side of the table. Whatever he returns, declarer will be able to draw trumps and lead a second heart, setting up a discard and making the contract. To beat the game you must rise with the ace on the

> **TOP TIP**
>
> It may seem obvious but to beat a major-suit game you need to score four tricks in defence! From the moment the dummy goes down, you must try to visualise how these four tricks can be scored. If partner needs to hold one or more particular cards, assume that he does hold those cards.

first round of hearts and then switch to the ◇J, establishing a fourth trick for the defence.

Here is another deal on the same theme — one where it was rather more difficult for West to judge the position.

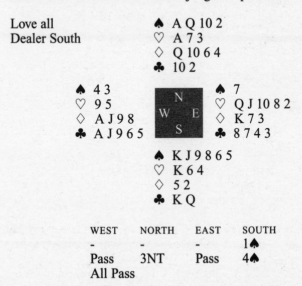

Love all
Dealer South

          ♠ A Q 10 2
          ♡ A 7 3
          ◇ Q 10 6 4
          ♣ 10 2

♠ 4 3   ♠ 7
♡ 9 5   ♡ Q J 10 8 2
◇ A J 9 8   ◇ K 7 3
♣ A J 9 6 5   ♣ 8 7 4 3

          ♠ K J 9 8 6 5
          ♡ K 6 4
          ◇ 5 2
          ♣ K Q

WEST	NORTH	EAST	SOUTH
-	-	-	1♠
Pass	3NT	Pass	4♠
All Pass			

North's 3NT showed a sound raise to game. With no interest in a slam, South was quick to sign off. Only one lead could threaten the contract and West found it — a heart. Declarer won with the king, drew trumps in two rounds and led a low diamond from his hand.

Fearing that declarer might hold the diamond king, West played low. Dummy's ten forced East's king and the contract could no longer be beaten. East set up a heart trick but he had no entry with which to enjoy it. Declarer won the second round of hearts with dummy's ace, returned to his hand with a trump and led another diamond. A shamefaced West rose with the ace and had no heart to play. Game made!

West should have risen with the ace on the first round of diamonds. He could then clear partner's heart trick while East still had the ◇K as an entry. There was little logic to West's fear that South might hold the ◇K. If he held ◇K-x or ◇K-x-x he would surely have led a low card from dummy, towards the king. Apart from that, South could not have a two-way guess in diamonds. If he needed to finesse the ◇10 to make ten tricks, he would do so.

On the next deal West has to foresee declarer's potential problems with communication. Take the West cards yourself and see how you would have fared.

Love all
Dealer East

		♠ 9 3 2	
		♡ 4 2	
		◇ A 8 7	
		♣ Q 10 9 7 5	

♠ J 10 6		♠ K 4
♡ A J 10 3	N	♡ K Q 6 5
◇ Q J 9 6 4	W E	◇ K 10 5 3
♣ 4	S	♣ K 3 2

	♠ A Q 8 7 5	
	♡ 9 8 7	
	◇ 2	
	♣ A J 8 6	

WEST	NORTH	EAST	SOUTH
-	-	1◇	1♠
Dble	2♠	3♡	Pass
4♡	Pass	Pass	4♠
All Pass			

The heart game would have failed and South's decision to sacrifice was a strange one. However... declarer won the diamond lead with dummy's ace and gave up a heart trick to East's queen. He ruffed the ◇K return and played another heart to West's ten. Over to you in the West seat. How would you continue?

Not realising that his next move was critical, West played another diamond. Declarer ruffed, reached dummy with a heart ruff and led ♣Q. East declined to cover, leaving this position:

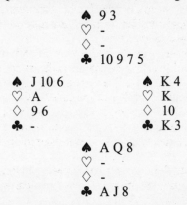

```
                    ♠ 9 3
                    ♡ -
                    ◇ -
                    ♣ 10 9 7 5

    ♠ J 10 6                    ♠ K 4
    ♡ A                         ♡ K
    ◇ 9 6                       ◇ 10
    ♣ -                         ♣ K 3

                    ♠ A Q 8
                    ♡ -
                    ◇ -
                    ♣ A J 8
```

Declarer now ran the ♣10. What could West do? If he ruffed, he would have to play a trump into South's tenace or a red card, which could be ruffed in the dummy, permitting a trump finesse. If instead he discarded, the lead would remain in dummy and declarer could take a trump finesse anyway. Ten tricks!

Where did the defence go wrong? It assisted declarer's cause for the diamond suit to be ruffed out. That was the reason why West had no safe return after ruffing a club. At the key moment West should have returned a third round of hearts instead of a diamond. If declarer played on clubs at that stage West would be able to ruff and exit safely in diamonds.

> **TOP TIP**
>
> Defenders often assist in the preparation for an elimination, by leading cards that declarer can ruff. Once you have taken the available winners in your suit, it may be best to switch elsewhere, perhaps to trumps. Another benefit of this is that you may leave yourself with a safe exit (in your original suit) later in the play.

On the next deal declarer arrives in a delicate 4-3 fit. He has communication problems and West needs to understand this in order to find the winning defence. It is no easy task, even then!

North-South game   ♠ A 2
Dealer North   ♡ K Q 10
                    ◇ Q J 10 9 6 4
                    ♣ K Q

♠ Q J 4	**N**	♠ K 10 8 7 5 3
♡ 8 6 4 3	**W E**	♡ 9 2
◇ A 2	**S**	◇ 7 5
♣ A 9 6 4		♣ 8 7 5

                    ♠ 9 6
                    ♡ A J 7 5
                    ◇ K 8 3
                    ♣ J 10 3 2

WEST	NORTH	EAST	SOUTH
-	1◇	Pass	1♡
Pass	3◇	Pass	4◇
Pass	4♡	All Pass	

Game in diamonds would have had no chance on a spade lead
and North-South did well to reach 4♡. Declarer ducked the spade
queen lead and won the spade continuation. Unwilling to rely on
a 3-3 trump break, he led the ♣K next. Take the West cards now.
You win with the ace of clubs and must calculate what to return.

Suppose you return a club to dummy's queen. Declarer will
draw two rounds of trumps and perhaps conclude from East's ♡9
that they are indeed breaking 4-2. In that case he will play a
diamond to the eight. This will leave you with no resource. If you
win and force dummy's last trump with a spade, declarer can
return to the ◇K to draw your trumps. If instead you duck,
declarer can cash his two good clubs and play another diamond
to your ace. Whether you play a spade or a trump now, he will
have the last three tricks. The play will follow similar lines if you
lead your last spade when you win with the ace of clubs.

Let's go back to Trick 4, just after you have taken the ♣A.
Once you can visualise declarer's entry problems and the fact
that he may need to enter his hand in diamonds, the winning
defence may (just) occur to you. You must underlead the
diamond ace, exiting with the ◇2! This gives declarer his entry
to hand before he can take advantage of it. If he plays another
diamond to your ace, for example, you will force the dummy
with your last spade and sit back, waiting for your trump trick.

Most defensive problems can be solved by a single technique
— thinking clearly! East went wrong on the next deal and had to
agree afterwards that there had really been no excuse.

Game all   ♠ -
Dealer West   ♡ A K Q 10 8
                      ◇ K Q J 9
                      ♣ A 9 8 3

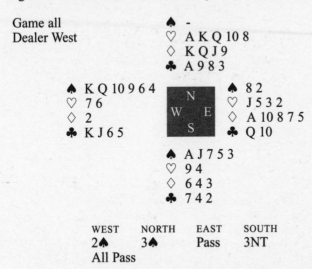

♠ K Q 10 9 6 4   ♠ 8 2
♡ 7 6   ♡ J 5 3 2
◇ 2   ◇ A 10 8 7 5
♣ K J 6 5   ♣ Q 10

                 ♠ A J 7 5 3
                 ♡ 9 4
                 ◇ 6 4 3
                 ♣ 7 4 2

WEST	NORTH	EAST	SOUTH
2♠	3♠	Pass	3NT
All Pass			

At the other table of a teams-of-four match, North had
doubled the weak two for take-out. South had passed for
penalties and picked up 200. Here North made a somewhat
unorthodox 3♠ overcall and South ended in 3NT.

West led the ♠K, asking for 'count or unblock'. A club was
thrown from dummy and East played the ♠8. Knowing from
East's failure to unblock an honour that South held the spade ace-
jack, West switched to a club. East won with the queen and…
Well, suppose you had been East. What would you have done?

Although he could see an end-play staring himself in the face,
East returned his remaining spade. South won gratefully with the
ace, throwing dummy's last low club. When he played a diamond
to the king, East ducked. The queen of diamonds was also
allowed to win. This brought East little comfort. Declarer cashed
the ♣A, removing East's last safe exit card, and played four
rounds of hearts, throwing East on lead. He had to play from his
◇A-10 to dummy's ◇J-9 and nine tricks were made.

Since all the assets needed for the end-play were on display in
the dummy, this was a poor effort by East. He should have
returned a club at Trick 3. Suppose declarer continues with two

rounds of diamonds, East ducking. These cards would remain:

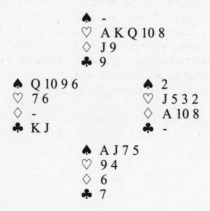

```
              ♠  -
              ♡  A K Q 10 8
              ◇  J 9
              ♣  9
♠ Q 10 9 6              ♠ 2
♡ 7 6                   ♡ J 5 3 2
◇ -                     ◇ A 10 8
♣ K J                  ♣ -
              ♠  A J 7 5
              ♡  9 4
              ◇  6
              ♣  7
```

Declarer plays four rounds of hearts, throwing East on lead. Since declarer has not been allowed to score the spade ace, the end-play does not bear sufficient fruit. East plays ace and another diamond, returning the lead to the dummy and West scores a club at Trick 13 to put the game one down.

On the next deal many East players would go wrong in the end position. How about you?

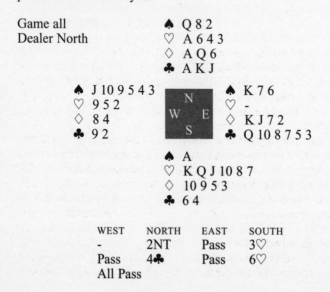

Game all
Dealer North

```
              ♠  Q 8 2
              ♡  A 6 4 3
              ◇  A Q 6
              ♣  A K J
♠ J 10 9 5 4 3     N       ♠ K 7 6
♡ 9 5 2        W     E     ♡ -
◇ 8 4              S       ◇ K J 7 2
♣ 9 2                      ♣ Q 10 8 7 5 3
              ♠  A
              ♡  K Q J 10 8 7
              ◇  10 9 5 3
              ♣  6 4
```

WEST	NORTH	EAST	SOUTH
-	2NT	Pass	3♡
Pass	4♣	Pass	6♡
All Pass			

The deal comes from rubber bridge and transfer responses were not being played. West led the ♠J against the small slam in hearts. Declarer won with the ace and played the king of trumps, drawing a club discard from East. The 3-0 trump break prevented him from eliminating both the black suits before playing on diamonds. (After drawing trumps and taking three black-suit ruffs, South's trumps would be exhausted.)

Declarer decided to eliminate the spade suit, nevertheless. He drew trumps, ending in the dummy, and ruffed a spade. He then crossed to the ♣A and took a second spade ruff. A finesse of the diamond queen lost to the king and East had to find an exit in this end position:

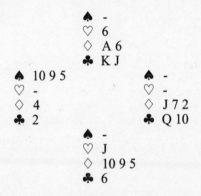

What would you have returned, sitting East?

The seemingly obvious diamond return would cost the contract. Declarer would win with the ◇10 and cross-ruff the remaining tricks. A club return, into dummy's tenace, is safe! From the evidence available to you in the East seat, how can you tell this?

Declarer is known to have four cards remaining in the minors. If he has three diamonds and one club, a diamond return is risky but a club return will ensure that you eventually score the ◇J. Suppose next that declarer is 2-2 in the minors. Again a club return will beat the contract, since declarer will have no way to eat his diamond loser. A club return will cost the contract only if declarer is now 1-3 in the minors. This is impossible because there are only two clubs out!

We will end the chapter with a splendid defence by Andrew Robson, playing in Amsterdam's Hoechst tournament. The key switch that he found was possible only by — you guessed it — reading declarer's mind. This was the deal:

Love all
Dealer South

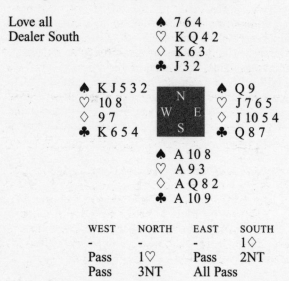

```
                    ♠ 7 6 4
                    ♡ K Q 4 2
                    ◇ K 6 3
                    ♣ J 3 2
  ♠ K J 5 3 2                    ♠ Q 9
  ♡ 10 8            N            ♡ J 7 6 5
  ◇ 9 7         W     E          ◇ J 10 5 4
  ♣ K 6 5 4         S            ♣ Q 8 7
                    ♠ A 10 8
                    ♡ A 9 3
                    ◇ A Q 8 2
                    ♣ A 10 9
```

WEST	NORTH	EAST	SOUTH
-	-	-	1◇
Pass	1♡	Pass	2NT
Pass	3NT	All Pass	

Robson led the ♠3 and East's queen was allowed to win. When the ♠9 was returned, declarer won with the ace and exited immediately with the ♠8. Suppose you had been West, holding Robson's cards. What would you have done next?

Declarer's intention was not difficult to divine. He hoped that West would cash his two spade winners. If East held length in both the red suits he would then be squeezed, either immediately or when declarer subsequently played his ♣A. Both Robson and the West player at the other table (where the play to the first three tricks had been identical) realised that they should not play their

TOP TIP

Suppose you are defending 3NT and have established some winners in the suit that was led. To your surprise declarer gives you the lead. Although it may seem obvious to cash your winners, this is often exactly what declarer wants you to do. The effect may be to squeeze your partner out of a guard on one of declarer's suits. Always think carefully before cashing four defensive tricks against 3NT. Even if you will never make the last trick in your suit, you may still gain by switching elsewhere. Reprieved of the squeeze, partner may score two tricks at the end.

spade winners. The next question was: what switch should they make?

West at the other table switched to the ♡10. Not the best! Martin, who was the declarer, won with dummy's king of hearts and promptly finessed his ♡9 for the contract. The same sort of thing might happen, should West switch to the ◇9. If declarer takes the card at face value, he can win in the dummy and take a deep finesse of the ◇8. It would not help East to split his ◇J-10 because declarer can cross to a heart to play on diamonds again.

Andrew Robson found the excellent switch to a low club, leaving declarer with no chance whatsoever. East's queen forced the ace and when neither red suit broke 3-3 the game was one down.

You may wonder how on earth Robson found this switch. Declarer had shown 18-19 points with his 2NT rebid. Surely there was a big risk that he might hold the ace and queen of clubs. Robson looked into declarer's mind. If he had a tenace in clubs, surely he would have cashed his red-suit winners before throwing West on lead. This would land the contract if West had nothing but clubs to lead when thrown in.

10
Surviving a Bad Trump Break

In this chapter we will look closely at some techniques you can use to overcome a bad trump division. We begin with a relatively straightforward deal where the best play in the trump suit depends on the lie of a key side suit.

Love all
Dealer South

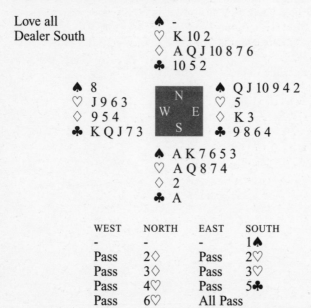

```
                ♠ -
                ♡ K 10 2
                ◊ A Q J 10 8 7 6
                ♣ 10 5 2
   ♠ 8                        ♠ Q J 10 9 4 2
   ♡ J 9 6 3      N           ♡ 5
   ◊ 9 5 4     W     E        ◊ K 3
   ♣ K Q J 7 3     S          ♣ 9 8 6 4
                ♠ A K 7 6 5 3
                ♡ A Q 8 7 4
                ◊ 2
                ♣ A
```

WEST	NORTH	EAST	SOUTH
-	-	-	1♠
Pass	2◊	Pass	2♡
Pass	3◊	Pass	3♡
Pass	4♡	Pass	5♣
Pass	6♡	All Pass	

Declarer won the club lead and played a diamond to the ace. He then called for the ◊Q, intending to run the card. If West won with the diamond king declarer would need a 3-2 trump break; he would draw trumps, ending in the dummy, and then play off the diamond suit. As the cards lay, East covered the diamond queen with the king. Declarer ruffed in his hand and saw that he no longer needed a 3-2 trump break. By employing a safety play in the trump suit, he could succeed also when West held four trumps.

Declarer cashed the ace of trumps at Trick 4 and continued with a trump to the ten. If the finesse had lost, trumps would have broken 3-2. It would then have been a simple matter to win the return and cross to dummy's king of trumps, pulling the last trump. When the trump finesse succeeded, East showing out, declarer reverted to diamonds. He discarded his spade losers and West could ruff when he liked. Declarer would win the return and play a trump to the king, drawing West's last trump.

Declarer went down on the next deal, although a skilled performer would have succeeded.

> **TOP TIP**
>
> When a defender has one more trump than the dummy, you can sometimes leave a master trump in dummy and run a long side suit. When the defender ruffs, you win his return and cross to dummy, drawing the last trump. You can then enjoy the rest of the side suit. This technique is called 'using a side suit as substitute trumps'.

Love all
Dealer North

♠ J 5 3 2
♡ A J 6
◇ K 8 7 4
♣ K 3

♠ K 10 9 7　　　　♠ -
♡ 9 8 3　　　　　♡ 10 7 4 2
◇ Q 10 2　　　　 ◇ J 9 6 3
♣ Q J 9　　　　　♣ 8 7 6 5 4

♠ A Q 8 6 4
♡ K Q 5
◇ A 5
♣ A 10 2

WEST	NORTH	EAST	SOUTH
-	1◇	Pass	1♠
Pass	2♠	Pass	6♠

South wasted little time in the auction. Unfortunately for him, he assigned just as few seconds to the play. He won the ♣Q lead with dummy's king and led a low trump, East showing out. There was no way to recover and the slam went one down. Would you have done any better?

On a deal like this, where the side suits are solid, there will be no excuse if you fail to plan for a bad trump break. You should win the club lead in your hand and lead a low trump towards dummy. If West shows out, you can pick up the trump suit for just one loser; dummy's jack will force the king and you can then lead twice towards your A-Q-8, finessing if East follows low.

On the present deal West will follow with the seven and dummy's jack will win, East showing out. What now? Prospects are hardly excellent but you will still succeed if you can strip West's side-suit cards and then end-play him in the trump suit. West's shape will need to be 4-3-3-3 or 4-3-4-2. After cashing dummy's club honour and the ace-king of diamonds, you ruff a diamond and play the king and queen of hearts. These cards will remain:

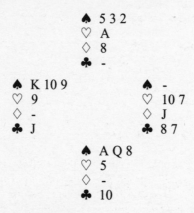

At this stage you must judge whether West's last minor-suit card is a diamond or a club. If it is a diamond, you will cross to the ♡A and ruff dummy's last diamond before exiting with the ♣10. In fact, it is a near certainty that West has another club. He would not lead from ♣Q-9 if he had ◇Q-J-10-2 available. (Even if West had discarded the ♣J, retaining the nine, the same inference would be available. A lead from ◇Q-J-10-2 would be more attractive than one from ♣Q-J doubleton.) You therefore ruff your last club, cash the ace of hearts and play a trump to the eight. It's time for West to give a helpless shrug of the shoulders.

Here's another one for you to try:

Game all
Dealer East

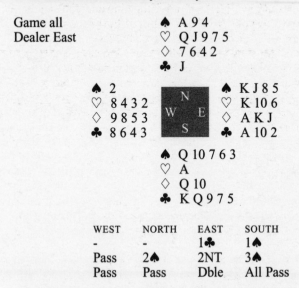

	WEST	NORTH	EAST	SOUTH
	-	-	1♣	1♠
	Pass	2♠	2NT	3♠
	Pass	Pass	Dble	All Pass

Deciding to lead from strength, West reaches for the ◇8. East scores the king and ace, noting the fall of South's queen. Take the East cards now. What would you have done next?

At the table East continued with the ◇J. Declarer ruffed, cashed the ♡A and played a club to the jack. East won with the ace and exited with a club, ruffed in the dummy. The ♡Q was covered by the king and ruffed. Declarer then ruffed another club and discarded his penultimate club on the ♡J. The lead was in dummy, with these cards still to be played:

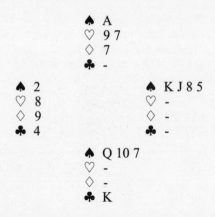

East had no answer to the next red card from dummy. If he ruffed with the king, declarer would discard his last club, win the trump return with dummy's ace and lead another red card towards his Q-10 of trumps. If instead East ruffed with a lower card, declarer would overruff, ruff the club king with the ace and again lead a plain card towards his last two trumps. Declarer had made the contract without scoring a trick from his K-Q-J of clubs!

Let's go back to Trick 3, just after East has taken his two diamond winners. A third round of diamonds can only help declarer to score the trumps in his hand. A stronger defence is for East to play ace and another club. This upsets declarer's timing, forcing him to use an entry to dummy — a club ruff — before the ♡A has been unblocked. If you can find a way to make the contract after this defence, we will refund you the cost of the book!

(Since you ask, we will admit we have used William Bailey's superb Deep Finesse computer program to check our analysis of the deal. Contrary to popular opinion, impecunious bridge writers cannot afford to hand out free books to all and sundry. No, we had to be sure we were right.)

We have seen already that adverse bidding can prove very helpful to declarer. On the next deal an Unusual No-trump overcall gave him early warning that the trumps might break poorly.

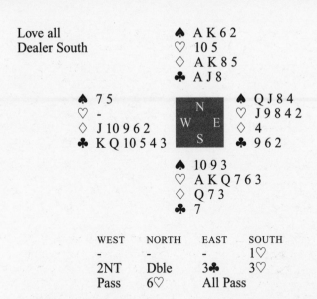

Love all
Dealer South

♠ A K 6 2
♡ 10 5
◇ A K 8 5
♣ A J 8

♠ 7 5
♡ -
◇ J 10 9 6 2
♣ K Q 10 5 4 3

♠ Q J 8 4
♡ J 9 8 4 2
◇ 4
♣ 9 6 2

♠ 10 9 3
♡ A K Q 7 6 3
◇ Q 7 3
♣ 7

WEST	NORTH	EAST	SOUTH
-	-	-	1♡
2NT	Dble	3♣	3♡
Pass	6♡	All Pass	

West led the ♣K, won in the dummy, and declarer's first problem was how to tackle the trump suit. Low to the ace will pick up the suit without loss when the jack is singleton. How about leading the ten on the first round, planning to run the card? If East covers with the jack and the nine or eight appears from East, you can return to dummy and finesse against East's remaining middle spot-card. Another advantage of leading the ten is that you can succeed even when East holds all five trumps!

Declarer led the ♡10 at Trick 2, covered by the jack and ace. When West showed out declarer returned to dummy with a spade and led a second trump. East played the eight and declarer won with the king. Declarer now had Q-7-6-3 in the trump suit against East's 9-4-2. He led the trump seven to East's nine and ruffed the club return.

Declarer had lost one trick and still had an apparent spade loser. It was clear from West's 2NT overall that he could be squeezed in the minors but the timing was delicate. Suppose declarer draws trumps at this stage, while the ♠K is still in dummy. He will go down! He will have to find a discard from a dummy that contains ♠K ◇A-K-8-5 ♣J. Instead, declarer must play a spade to the king, return to the queen of diamonds and only then play his remaining trumps. This will be the position when the last trump is played:

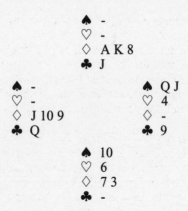

Now the last trump catches West in a positional simple squeeze, forcing him to surrender a twelfth trick.

On the next deal declarer succeeded in his contract of 3♡ doubled, overcoming a bad trump break. Watch as the play is described and see if you can spot two ways in which the defenders might have beaten the contract.

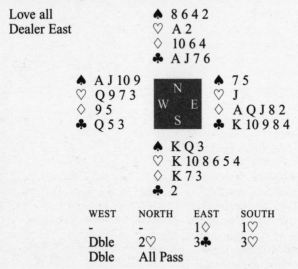

WEST	NORTH	EAST	SOUTH
-	-	1♢	1♡
Dble	2♡	3♣	3♡
Dble	All Pass		

It was unclear to West how strong his partner might be for the 3♣ rebid. (Some players use a Good-Bad 2NT in this situation. A 2NT rebid shows any minimum hand with the shape to compete. A rebid of 3♣ or 3♢ would be full strength.) Anyway,

West risked a penalty double of 3♡ and launched the defence with the ◇9.

East won with the ace and returned the diamond queen to declarer's king. A possible line now was to play East for the ♠A, using dummy's two aces to lead towards South's spade holding. However, West might well have led a club, holding king-queen in the suit, so his final double made him a strong favourite to hold the spade ace.

Declarer embarked on a different line — to score as many trumps as possible in his own hand. He crossed to the ace of clubs and ruffed a club. A trump to the ace, the jack falling from East, was followed by a second club ruff. Declarer now exited with the spade king, relieved to see that West did indeed hold the ace of that suit. The ♠J return was taken with the queen and declarer exited with a third round of spades, leaving these cards still out:

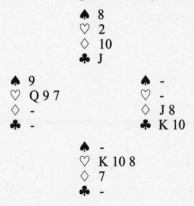

```
                ♠ 8
                ♡ 2
                ◇ 10
                ♣ J

    ♠ 9                      ♠ -
    ♡ Q 9 7                  ♡ -
    ◇ -                      ◇ J 8
    ♣ -                      ♣ K 10

                ♠ -
                ♡ K 10 8
                ◇ 7
                ♣ -
```

West exited with the ♠9 and declarer ruffed with the eight. When he played a diamond, West had to ruff his partner's winner and lead into declarer's K-10 of trumps. Declarer therefore scored one winner in each side suit and the equivalent of six trump tricks in his hand (dummy's ace won one of the tricks, in fact). So, how could the defenders have done better?

TOP TIP

When you have long trumps and the suit breaks badly, you can often fare surprisingly well by taking ruffs in the long trump hand. Suppose you hold A-x in dummy and K-J-10-x-x-x in your hand. You play the ace and finesse the jack, your left-hand-opponent showing out. If you can score two ruffs in your hand you will be able to exit near the end, certain to score the remaining K-10 of trumps.

One difficult chance was for East to play the $\diamondsuit$J at Trick 1. The defenders could not then have been deprived of two spade tricks, two diamond tricks and one trick in the trump suit (only one because declarer can always end-play West). However, West's final double suggested to East that the $\diamondsuit$9 might be a singleton. In that case, playing the jack at Trick 1 would not work well.

A much more obvious chance arose in the end position shown in our diagram. West should have exited with a trump instead of a spade. Declarer wins and exits with a diamond but West can throw the $\spadesuit$9 and the defenders score two more tricks.

Let's see one more deal where the winning technique is to aim to score all the trumps in the long-trump hand. Blissfully unaware of this, the original declarer set off on a different line.

```
Love all                  ♠ -
Dealer North              ♡ 9 5 4
                          ◇ A J 7 6 5 4
                          ♣ A 10 8 6

        ♠ Q                             ♠ 10 9 7 6 2
        ♡ Q J 10 8 3         N          ♡ A K 7 6
        ◇ K 9 3          W       E      ◇ 8 2
        ♣ Q J 7 2           S          ♣ K 3

                          ♠ A K J 8 5 4 3
                          ♡ 2
                          ◇ Q 10
                          ♣ 9 5 4
```

WEST	NORTH	EAST	SOUTH
-	1$\diamondsuit$	Pass	1$\spadesuit$
Pass	2$\diamondsuit$	Pass	4$\spadesuit$

You wouldn't open on those North cards? No, but you know one or two people who would, we're sure. West led the $\heartsuit$Q and persisted with the suit, declarer ruffing the second round. When the ace of trumps dropped the queen from West the adverse trump break was apparent. Declarer continued with the $\diamondsuit$Q, covered by the king and ace, and returned to his hand with the $\diamondsuit$10. After a club to the ace he tried his luck with the $\diamondsuit$J, hoping that East would follow. Not today. East ruffed with the ten and the contract was one down, whether declarer overruffed or discarded.

Ten tricks can be made if declarer aims to score all his trumps. He ruffs the second heart and plays the trump ace as before, dropping West's queen. On this trick he throws a diamond from dummy, preserving the losing heart. The queen of diamonds is covered by the king and ace and declarer takes advantage of the entry to dummy by ruffing the heart that he retained. The ten of diamonds is overtaken by the jack, leaving declarer in dummy with these cards still out:

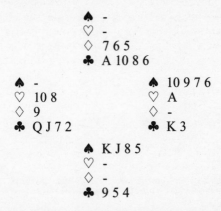

East has no constructive move available when a diamond is led from dummy. If he ruffs with the ten, declarer will throw a losing club. He can then win the club return (as good as anything for the defence) and lead another diamond. If East ruffs again declarer will discard his last club loser and claim the balance. If instead East discards, declarer will ruff with the ♠5 and exit in clubs, certain to score his K-J-8 of trumps over East's remaining 9-7-6. The play is similar if East chooses not to ruff the third round of diamonds.

Does anything else occur to you about that deal? West's heart continuation at Trick 2 was helpful to declarer, allowing him to score a low trump without employing an entry to dummy. It was difficult indeed for West to diagnose the situation. However, had he switched to any black card (dangerous as this looks), or even to the ◇K, declarer would have gone down. Perhaps bridge-playing computers of the future will be capable of such defences.

We will end the chapter with an amusing deal that arose in a teams event in the Mayfair Bridge Club. Martin was partnering his wife, Audrey, and their team-mates were G.C.H.Fox (known universally as 'Foxy') and his wife Betty.

Game all
Dealer North

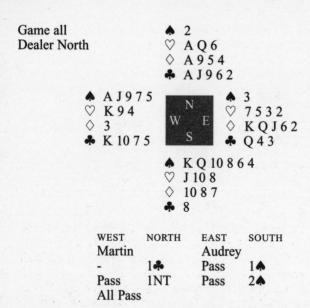

```
                    ♠ 2
                    ♡ A Q 6
                    ◇ A 9 5 4
                    ♣ A J 9 6 2
    ♠ A J 9 7 5                   ♠ 3
    ♡ K 9 4          N            ♡ 7 5 3 2
    ◇ 3          W       E        ◇ K Q J 6 2
    ♣ K 10 7 5        S           ♣ Q 4 3
                    ♠ K Q 10 8 6 4
                    ♡ J 10 8
                    ◇ 10 8 7
                    ♣ 8
```

WEST	NORTH	EAST	SOUTH
Martin		Audrey	
-	1♣	Pass	1♠
Pass	1NT	Pass	2♠
All Pass			

Martin led his singleton diamond against the unambitious contract of 2♠ and Audrey won with the jack. When the diamond king was returned, Martin ruffed and switched to a low club. Declarer rose with the ace and played a trump to the king and ace. Martin now shifted to the ♡9. If a heart finesse were to lose, another diamond ruff would follow and declarer might go down when trumps had started 3-3 (East holding J-x-x). Declarer can hardly be blamed for rising with the ace of hearts. He crossed to his hand with a club ruff and played the queen of trumps. Six losers could not thereafter be avoided and he finished one down in his part-score.

It's hard to imagine how the bidding went at the other table but Foxy somehow arrived in 4♠. West hazarded a double and led his singleton diamond. Foxy won with the ace of diamonds, cashed the club ace and ruffed a club. The jack of hearts was covered by the king and ace and he ruffed another club in his hand. The ten and queen of hearts stood up and a further club ruff left declarer in the South hand with these cards outstanding:

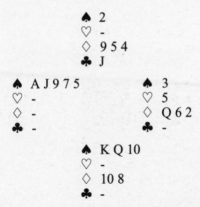

Needing two more tricks, Foxy exited in diamonds. West had to ruff and his trump return allowed declarer to claim the contract. As the cards lay, declarer could also have succeeded by exiting with the trump king in the above end position. Do you see why a diamond exit was superior? Suppose West had instead started with four spades and two diamonds. The end position would have been:

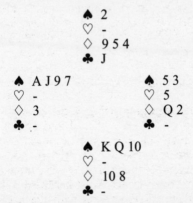

If declarer plays the trump king in this position West can defeat the contract by ducking. Declarer cannot afford to play another trump. When he tries a diamond instead, East will win and lead a trump through declarer's tenace to beat the contract.

Foxy's preferred diamond exit works in both situations. Here East will win and play a trump. Declarer rises with the king and it does West no good to duck now. Declarer would simply exit with another diamond, forcing West to ruff and return a trump.

11
Avoidance Play

The term 'avoidance play' sounds very grand but it means little more than taking steps to keep a dangerous defender off lead. There is nothing very difficult about our first example of the technique but many players would go down, you can be sure.

East-West game
Dealer North

North
♠ 10 2
♡ A J 9 4
♢ A Q 2
♣ Q 10 7 6

West
♠ Q 9 8 6
♡ 3 2
♢ J 9 8 5
♣ 9 5 2

East
♠ K 7 5 4
♡ K 5
♢ K 10 6 4
♣ A 8 4

South
♠ A J 3
♡ Q 10 8 7 6
♢ 7 3
♣ K J 3

WEST	NORTH	EAST	SOUTH
-	1♣	Pass	1♡
Pass	2♡	Pass	4♡
All Pass			

West leads the ♠6 to East's king. How will you play?

You win East's ♠K with the ace and… Do you? If so, you will go down! A trump finesse will lose and East will return a spade to West's queen. A diamond switch will then set up a fourth trick for the defence before you have established a discard on the clubs.

Nor is it any better to play on clubs before drawing trumps, because you cannot enjoy a discard on the club suit until trumps have been drawn. The only way to succeed is to duck East's king of spades at Trick 1. By doing so, you prevent West from gaining the lead later. East cannot attack diamonds from his side of the table. You win his return and take the trump finesse. It loses but again East cannot play on diamonds. You will be able to draw trumps and set up a discard on the clubs.

When you are in a 5-4 fit and the opposing trumps break 2-2, you wouldn't think that you could run into trouble in the trump suit. Unless you play well on the following hand, you will!

> **TOP TIP**
>
> Always consider carefully before winning with an ace at Trick 1. By holding up, you may be able to restrict the defenders' communications. This is well known in no-trumps, when you have such as A-x-x facing x-x and wish to exhaust one defender's holding. A hold-up can be just as important in a suit contract. By ducking the first round you may prevent the defenders from crossing in this suit later in the play.

North-South game
Dealer East

```
                  ♠ 10 9 7 6 4
                  ♡ K 4 3 2
                  ◇ 7 3
                  ♣ 9 2
  ♠ J 3                        ♠ 8 5
  ♡ 10 9 8 5        N          ♡ A Q J 7
  ◇ J 8          W   E         ◇ K 10 9
  ♣ 10 8 6 5 3      S          ♣ A Q J 7
                  ♠ A K Q 2
                  ♡ 6
                  ◇ A Q 6 5 4 2
                  ♣ K 4
```

WEST	NORTH	EAST	SOUTH
-	-	1♣	1◇
Pass	Pass	1NT	2♠
Pass	3♠	Pass	4♠
All Pass			

Many players would bid a second time on those East cards but he might have asked himself: Where are the spades?

East soon found out where the spades were and West led the ♡10 against the opponents' game in that suit. The ten won the first trick and declarer ruffed the heart continuation, proceeding to draw trumps in two rounds. Take the South cards now. What would you do next?

The original declarer led a low diamond from his hand. West defended strongly by rising with the jack, ensuring that he won the trick. A third round of hearts forced declarer's last trump and when the ◇K did not fall under declarer's ace the game was one down. Ruffing the diamonds good would not help because when he led a club towards the king East would rise with the ace and cash a heart.

Declarer could not afford West to gain the lead and should have led the ◇Q instead of a low diamond. East surely held the ◇K and would not be able to play on hearts effectively from his side of the table. On any return, declarer could ruff the diamonds good and return to his hand to enjoy them.

On the next deal declarer needs to eliminate clubs to prepare for an end-play. Contrary to what you might expect from the diagram, there is a right and a wrong way to play the club suit.

TOP TIP

Suppose you are in a trump contract and have a side suit such as K-x-x opposite a singleton in dummy. You would like to lead the suit from dummy, of course, but this is not always possible. Forced to lead from your own hand, you should consider if there is any benefit in leading the king. Only the defender with the ace can now win the trick and perhaps from his side of the table he will not be able to lead trumps safely.

Love all
Dealer South

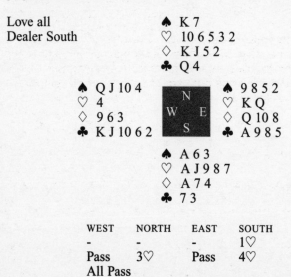

```
                    ♠ K 7
                    ♡ 10 6 5 3 2
                    ◇ K J 5 2
                    ♣ Q 4
  ♠ Q J 10 4                      ♠ 9 8 5 2
  ♡ 4              N              ♡ K Q
  ◇ 9 6 3       W     E           ◇ Q 10 8
  ♣ K J 10 6 2     S              ♣ A 9 8 5
                    ♠ A 6 3
                    ♡ A J 9 8 7
                    ◇ A 7 4
                    ♣ 7 3
```

WEST	NORTH	EAST	SOUTH
-	-	-	1♡
Pass	3♡	Pass	4♡
All Pass			

An inexperienced player would say to himself: 'Not so bad. It's all on the diamond finesse.' However, if you can eliminate the black suits there is a chance of end-playing East on the second round of trumps. Suppose you win the spade lead in dummy and lead the queen or four of clubs. You will go down against alert defence. West can gain the lead twice in clubs and will be able to lead a diamond each time, setting up East's queen before you have a chance to throw him in.

Instead you should play the king and ace of spades and lead a club towards dummy's queen. This is an avoidance play to prevent West from gaining the lead twice in the suit. Suppose he rises with the king on the first round of clubs and switches to a diamond. You will win with the ace and play a second club to the queen and ace. East cannot continue diamonds from his side. Let's say he plays the king of trumps instead. You win with the ace, ruff your last spade and throw East in with a trump. He must lead into dummy's ◇K-J or play a black suit, giving you a ruff-and-discard.

The fact that one defender is dangerous, the other safe, often affects your play in the trump suit. To keep the dangerous defender off lead you may opt to finesse against a missing trump queen instead of playing for the drop. Look at this deal:

> **TOP TIP**
>
> When you hold Q-x opposite x-x, it may seem irrelevant how you play the suit. By leading towards the queen, you reduce the chance that your left-hand-opponent (perhaps the more dangerous defender) can gain the lead twice. The same is true with K-10 opposite x-x when you know the ace lies over the king. Lead towards the honours, intending to play the 10 and you keep left-hand opponent off lead, unless he holds both the queen and jack.

East-West game
Dealer South

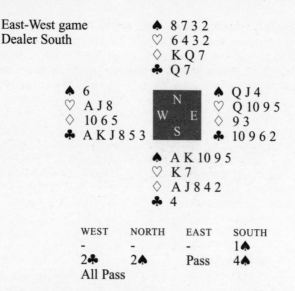

♠ 8 7 3 2
♡ 6 4 3 2
◇ K Q 7
♣ Q 7

♠ 6
♡ A J 8
◇ 10 6 5
♣ A K J 8 5 3

♠ Q J 4
♡ Q 10 9 5
◇ 9 3
♣ 10 9 6 2

♠ A K 10 9 5
♡ K 7
◇ A J 8 4 2
♣ 4

WEST	NORTH	EAST	SOUTH
-	-	-	1♠
2♣	2♠	Pass	4♠
All Pass			

West plays his two top clubs and you ruff the second round. How would you continue?

You can afford to lose a trump trick but not to East, since he could switch to a heart through the king. At Trick 3 you should cross to the king of diamonds. You then lead a trump, intending to finesse the ten. East may well play low, in case his partner has a singleton honour. In that case the ten will win and you will end with an overtrick. If East does choose to split his honours, you will win with the ace and return to dummy with a second diamond to repeat the finesse. There is little risk involved in playing a second round of diamonds. It is barely possible, on the bidding, that East holds two trumps and only one diamond. If West were to ruff the second diamond, you would still make the contract.

TOP TIP

When you need to keep one opponent off lead, this will often affect how you play the trump suit. With A-J-x-x-x opposite K-10-x-x, you may choose to finesse, to prevent the dangerous defender gaining the lead with Q-x-x. Similarly, with K-J-x-x-x opposite A-x-x you may choose to play the ace and king, in case the dangerous defender holds Q-x over the jack.

The most common setting of avoidance play is in no-trumps, when one defender has tricks to cash but the link between the two defenders has been broken. How would you have fared in this 3NT contract?

Game all
Dealer East

```
                    ♠ 6 5
                    ♡ 8 7 4 3
                    ◇ A Q 3
                    ♣ 9 6 5 4
    ♠ 8 4 2                        ♠ K Q J 10 7
    ♡ 10 9 6          N            ♡ K J 5
    ◇ 9 8 7 5 4   W       E        ◇ J 6
    ♣ 10 8            S            ♣ Q J 7
                    ♠ A 9 3
                    ♡ A Q 2
                    ◇ K 10 2
                    ♣ A K 3 2
```

WEST	NORTH	EAST	SOUTH
-	-	1♠	Dble
Pass	2♡	Pass	2NT
Pass	3NT	All Pass	

West led a spade and declarer held up until the third round, breaking the link between the defenders. He could count eight tricks, assuming the heart finesse was right, and therefore needed a third trick from the club suit. How would you have continued?

The obvious chance in clubs is that West holds three cards in the suit. He will then have to win the third round and the danger hand will not gain the lead. There is another chance — that East holds three clubs including the seven!

After winning the third spade, you cross to the queen of diamonds and lead the ♣4. When the ♣7 appears on your right, you play low from the South hand, confident that West will have to overtake. Sure enough, West overtakes with the eight and a club trick has been ducked into the safe hand. Nine tricks result when clubs break 3-2 and the heart finesse succeeds. It would do East no good to split his honours on

> **TOP TIP**
>
> When the dangerous defender holds the lowest outstanding spot-card in the suit, you can duck the trick to his partner when this card appears. Lead through the dangerous defender, waiting until he chooses to play his lowest card. You can then play low from the next hand.

the first round. You would win with the ace, cross back to dummy with a diamond and lead another club. East has to play the seven this time or you will make four club tricks. You play low from your hand and, once again, West has to overtake.

The theme is the similar on the next 3NT — one defender is safe, the other dangerous. The original declarer played carelessly.

North-South game
Dealer South

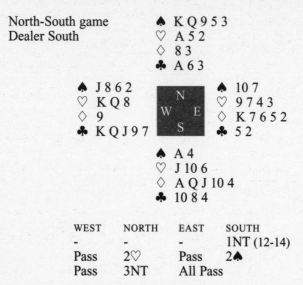

```
                    ♠ K Q 9 5 3
                    ♡ A 5 2
                    ◇ 8 3
                    ♣ A 6 3
  ♠ J 8 6 2                        ♠ 10 7
  ♡ K Q 8           N             ♡ 9 7 4 3
  ◇ 9           W       E         ◇ K 7 6 5 2
  ♣ K Q J 9 7       S             ♣ 5 2
                    ♠ A 4
                    ♡ J 10 6
                    ◇ A Q J 10 4
                    ♣ 10 8 4
```

WEST	NORTH	EAST	SOUTH
-	-	-	1NT (12-14)
Pass	2♡	Pass	2♠
Pass	3NT	All Pass	

A transfer sequence left South in 3NT and West led the ♣K. Declarer held up dummy's club ace for two rounds and won the third round. A diamond to the queen won the next trick and he continued with the ace of spades and a spade to the king. A 3-3 break in either spades or diamonds would have seen the contract home but Lady Luck was in a bad mood. East showed out on the third round of spades and West then showed out when the diamond finesse was repeated.

'I did all I could,' said declarer with a sad shake of the head.

Did you spot where he went wrong?

On the second round of spades, declarer should have inserted dummy's nine, ducking a trick to the safe hand. He could then have scored four spades, three diamonds and two aces. It's the sort of hand where a good fraction of contestants in a pairs field would end up saying: 'How on earth did I miss that?'

On the next deal declarer needed several ruffs in the dummy and therefore had to keep the defender with the last trump off lead. His first problem was to decide which defender held the last trump!

> **TOP TIP**
>
> In side suits, as well as in the trump suit, the safety of your contract can be enhanced by ducking a round to the safe defender. Suppose you hold A-K-10-x-x in dummy opposite your Q-8. By playing low to the eight on the first round you may be able to keep the right-hand defender off lead. If instead you cash the queen and finesse the ten on the second round, you improve your chance of keeping the left-hand defender off lead.

North-South game
Dealer South

```
                    ♠ 8 7 5 4 2
                    ♡ 8 3
                    ◇ 7 2
                    ♣ 10 9 6 2
  ♠ K J 9 6                        ♠ A Q 10 3
  ♡ Q 6 5 4          N             ♡ J 10 9
  ◇ K 9 8 4       W     E          ◇ Q J 6 5
  ♣ 7                S             ♣ 8 3
                    ♠ -
                    ♡ A K 7 2
                    ◇ A 10 3
                    ♣ A K Q J 5 4
```

WEST	NORTH	EAST	SOUTH
-	-	-	2♣
Pass	2◇	Pass	3♣
Pass	4♣	Pass	6♣
All Pass			

Take the South cards yourself. West finds the only lead to trouble your slam, a trump. East follows with the ♣3 and you win with the ace. To bring the total to twelve, you will need to score three ruffs in the dummy. Ruffing two hearts will be no problem but you will have to surrender the lead before you can ruff a diamond. If the defender with the last trump gains the lead he will spoil your plans by removing dummy's last trump. How will you play the hand?

First of all, you must diagnose which defender holds the missing trump. Most players would lead the eight from 8-7, so East probably holds the missing trump. You cash the two top hearts and ruff a heart with the ten. You next lead a diamond from dummy, intending to play the ten and duck the trick to West (the safe hand, who does not hold the last trump).

Let's suppose that East is a sharp customer, who thwarts you by inserting the diamond queen. You win with the ace and lead your fourth heart. By good fortune it is West who follows with the last heart. You discard a diamond from dummy! West has no trump to play, so nothing can prevent you from ruffing two diamonds in dummy. By swapping a heart ruff for a diamond ruff, you keep the danger hand off lead.

On the next deal the declarer, Marcin Leisnecki, was forced to make various assumptions about the lie of the defenders' cards. The cards did indeed lie as he required but few players would have seen the winning play. (There's a chance for you to feel smug now, by making the contract yourself.)

East-West game
Dealer South

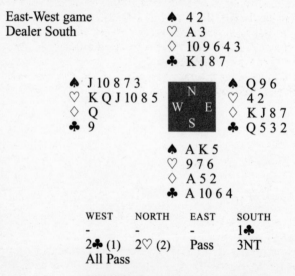

```
                    ♠ 4 2
                    ♡ A 3
                    ◇ 10 9 6 4 3
                    ♣ K J 8 7
♠ J 10 8 7 3                        ♠ Q 9 6
♡ K Q J 10 8 5        N              ♡ 4 2
◇ Q              W         E         ◇ K J 8 7
♣ 9                  S              ♣ Q 5 3 2
                    ♠ A K 5
                    ♡ 9 7 6
                    ◇ A 5 2
                    ♣ A 10 6 4
```

WEST	NORTH	EAST	SOUTH
-	-	-	1♣
2♣ (1)	2♡ (2)	Pass	3NT
All Pass			

(1) Michaels cue-bid, at least 5-5 in the majors.
(2) Sound club raise with a heart stopper.

West leads the king of hearts against 3NT. Would you have seen any chance of making nine tricks? Yes, we know you would never have bid such a poor contract!

Declarer needed to score more than one diamond trick and would therefore have to surrender the lead before establishing nine tricks. The first necessary assumption was that West held six hearts to East's two. It would then be safe to lose the lead to East. Since West's overcall had promised a major two-suiter, his most likely shape (including six hearts) was 5-6-1-1. If the diamond singleton was an honour, it might be possible to end-play East in the suit, forcing him to surrender a trick to dummy's ◇10.

One big problem remained. Before East could be end-played in diamonds, he would have to be stripped of his holdings in the other suits. How could his spades be removed? This would be possible only if East held three spades to the queen. By leading spades twice towards his hand – an avoidance play – declarer could ensure that the spade trick was ducked to the safe (East) hand.

Leisnecki won the second round of hearts and led a spade from dummy. East played low and declarer won with the ace. Returning to dummy with the king of clubs, Leisnecki next led the jack of clubs. When East declined to cover he unblocked the ten from his hand. The ♣8 was run next (it would make no difference if East were to cover at any stage), followed by a second round of spades. East chose to play the queen on this trick and the card was allowed to hold.

Declarer won the spade return and cashed the ♣A. He had reached this desirable end position:

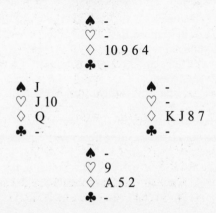

Ace and another diamond threw East on lead and dummy's ◇10 scored the last trick to give declarer his game. Brilliant play, yes?

We will end the chapter with a deal from a Summer Nationals in Las Vegas. Martin was partnering Dr Lilian Reich in the Lifemaster Pairs and the opponents were Dorothy Truscott and Gail Greenberg, two big names from the USA's Hall of Fame.

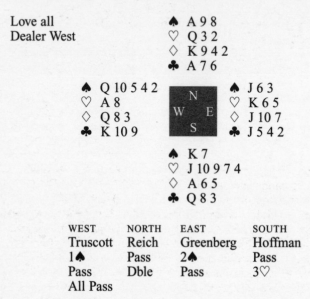

Love all
Dealer West

	♠ A 9 8	
	♡ Q 3 2	
	◇ K 9 4 2	
	♣ A 7 6	

♠ Q 10 5 4 2		♠ J 6 3
♡ A 8		♡ K 6 5
◇ Q 8 3		◇ J 10 7
♣ K 10 9		♣ J 5 4 2

	♠ K 7	
	♡ J 10 9 7 4	
	◇ A 6 5	
	♣ Q 8 3	

WEST	NORTH	EAST	SOUTH
Truscott	Reich	Greenberg	Hoffman
1♠	Pass	2♠	Pass
Pass	Dble	Pass	3♡
All Pass			

A spade was led and Martin won in hand with the king (essential on certain lines of play). The ten of trumps ran to East's king and a key moment of the deal had already been reached. Suppose you had held those East cards. What would you return?

Greenberg chose to return a spade, after which it was easy for Martin to draw trumps and set up a diamond for a club discard. Nine tricks were made.

Suppose instead that East switches to clubs, aiming to set up a winner or two in that suit before declarer can establish a discard. The best card is the jack of clubs. Do you see why? If you switch to a low club instead and the nine is allowed to win, West may be tempted to continue the suit.

The contract can still be made after a switch to the ♣J but only by accurate play. Declarer must win with the ♣A, cross to the ◇A and lead the ♠7. When West splits her Q-10, declarer can either duck or win with the spade ace and return the ♠9, ditching a diamond. After the latter play West will be on lead with these cards left:

```
              ♠ -
              ♡ Q 3
              ◊ K 9 4
              ♣ 7 6
  ♠ 5 2                    ♠ -
  ♡ A                      ♡ 6 5
  ◊ Q 8                    ◊ J 10
  ♣ K 10                   ♣ 5 4 2
              ♠ -
              ♡ J 9 7 4
              ◊ 6
              ♣ Q 8
```

Declarer cannot be prevented from ruffing a diamond good for a club discard. If West tries a spade, for example, he will ruff with dummy's queen and throw a club from his hand. The loser-on-loser avoidance play, throwing a diamond on the third round of spades, lets him set up the diamonds without allowing East on lead to play a club.

When Martin had finished explaining this line, at his usual machine-gun rate, Gail Greenberg had her answer ready: 'I didn't want to give you the chance for such a brilliancy!'

TOP TIP

On the Las Vegas deal West's opening bid announced that she held five spades. Suppose instead that East-West had not bid and this was the spade lay-out:

```
              ♠ A-K-8
  ♠ Q-10-5-4-2        ♠ J-6-3
              ♠ 9-7
```

West leads the ♠4 and dummy wins. It may be important for the defenders to know if they can eventually establish a spade trick. East should signal his count with the ♠3, letting West know that there is no spade trick to come. East should also observe the spot-card dropped by declarer. Here he will follow with the ♠7 and it is a fair assumption that the ♠2 lies with West, giving her five spades. A top-class declarer may false-card from 9-7-2 but very few players are up to it.

12

Defending the Squeeze

What personal qualities do you need to defend competently against a potential squeeze? Of course, you must be able to think clearly and to put in the hard work of counting — both points and distribution. These attributes are necessary when defending any type of contract. The required 'extra' here is that you should understand the squeeze from declarer's point of view.

To prepare for most squeezes, declarer needs to rectify the count (to lose at an early stage those tricks that he can afford to lose). The defenders must be wary of assisting this process. Many squeezes succeed because the defenders thoughtlessly take their 'book', tightening the end position for declarer. Although you could not call it a rule, you should certainly think twice before cashing four tricks against 3NT when you cannot see where a fifth trick will come from. Look at the defence on this deal:

```
North-South game        ♠ 9 2
Dealer South            ♡ K 7 6 4
                        ◇ K 10 6 4
                        ♣ A 6 4

   ♠ K 10 7 3                        ♠ A Q 6 5
   ♡ J 9 5 3          N              ♡ 10 8
   ◇ Q 9 3         W     E           ◇ J 8 2
   ♣ 10 2             S              ♣ J 9 8 5

                        ♠ J 8 4
                        ♡ A Q 2
                        ◇ A 7 5
                        ♣ K Q 7 3
```

WEST	NORTH	EAST	SOUTH
-	-	-	1NT (15-17)
Pass	2♣	Pass	2◇
Pass	3NT	All Pass	

At one table of a teams-of-four match West was deterred from a major-suit lead by North's Stayman bid. He led the ♣10 and declarer simply tested hearts and clubs in turn, going down when neither suit broke 3-3.

At the other table West led a spade, seemingly a better start, and the defenders blithely took four tricks in the suit. Declarer threw a diamond and a club from dummy, a diamond from his hand. He won the ♣10 switch with the ace and cashed three hearts. On the third round East had to retain his clubs and therefore threw a diamond. Declarer cashed the ♣K, leaving these cards still out:

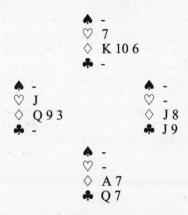

When the club queen was played West was squeezed in the red suits. It had been a non-simultaneous double squeeze. Both defenders were squeezed but not on the same trick.

The ending was possible only because the defenders had taken their four spade tricks. Taking three of the four tricks does no damage. Suppose the defenders then switch to a heart. The game will go down. If declarer plays three rounds of hearts, as before, East can pitch a diamond. Three rounds of clubs will not then squeeze West because he can throw his last spade.

On the next deal, from rubber bridge, declarer made his

doubled contract with the aid of a strip squeeze. Watch as the play is described and see if you can spot where West missed his chance.

North-South game
Dealer South

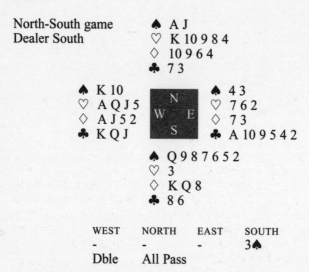

♠ A J
♡ K 10 9 8 4
◇ 10 9 6 4
♣ 7 3

♠ K 10
♡ A Q J 5
◇ A J 5 2
♣ K Q J

♠ 4 3
♡ 7 6 2
◇ 7 3
♣ A 10 9 5 4 2

♠ Q 9 8 7 6 5 2
♡ 3
◇ K Q 8
♣ 8 6

WEST	NORTH	EAST	SOUTH
-	-	-	3♠
Dble	All Pass		

Yes, there are still some players who play penalty doubles of three-bids! West led the king of clubs, winning the first trick, and continued with the jack of clubs to East's ace. Back came the ◇7 to the king and ace and West now had to choose an exit card. He could not afford to play a diamond from the jack and playing on hearts would give declarer a discard for his losing diamond. A third club, giving a ruff-and-discard would not concede the contract directly, but it would give declarer an entry to his hand. He could then lead a heart towards the king while the trump entry to dummy was intact.

If West exited with the ♠10 declarer would overtake dummy's jack with the queen and again set up a heart. West eventually decided to exit with the ♠K to dummy's ace. Declarer could not cross to the ◇Q now, to lead a heart, because this would set up West's ◇J. Instead he overtook the trump jack with the queen and ran the trump suit. This end position arose:

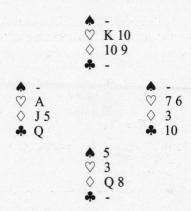

The last trump caught West in a strip squeeze. A red-suit discard would surrender a trick immediately. If instead he threw his last club he would be thrown in with the ♡A to concede two diamond tricks. Did you spot the mistake that West made?

West should not have captured the first round of diamonds, leaving himself with a vulnerable J-x holding. Had he ducked instead, he would hold a major tenace (A-J) over declarer's queen. Declarer would then have no resource. If he led a heart towards the king before drawing trumps, West would rise with the ace and give his partner a diamond ruff. Nor would a strip squeeze (reducing West to ♡A ♢A-J) be possible. That's because declarer cannot run the trump suit; two rounds of trumps would strand him in the dummy.

It's time for a deal where the defenders can attack the threat cards that declarer needs for a squeeze to succeed. If you are not exhausted by this stage of the book (perhaps it was unwise of you to read it all at one sitting), test yourself by taking the East cards.

> ### TOP TIP
> When you hold A-J-x over dummy's K-Q-10, there are several reasons why you may choose not to win the king with the ace. If you capture you cannot continue the suit; duck instead and you will score two tricks if partner gains the lead and plays the suit. A different reason is that a first-round capture will force you to retain a guard of J-x against dummy's Q-10. You may then be liable to a throw-in. A holding of A-J over the queen, after a duck on the first round, is not so dangerous. You may be able to throw the jack at a late stage, avoiding any intended throw-in.

North-South game
Dealer South

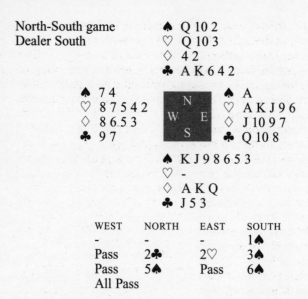

♠ Q 10 2
♡ Q 10 3
◇ 4 2
♣ A K 6 4 2

West:
♠ 7 4
♡ 8 7 5 4 2
◇ 8 6 5 3
♣ 9 7

East:
♠ A
♡ A K J 9 6
◇ J 10 9 7
♣ Q 10 8

South:
♠ K J 9 8 6 5 3
♡ -
◇ A K Q
♣ J 5 3

WEST	NORTH	EAST	SOUTH
-	-	-	1♠
Pass	2♣	2♡	3♠
Pass	5♠	Pass	6♠
All Pass			

West led the ♡4 (not our choice from a holding of five small) and declarer played low from the dummy. East played the nine and declarer ruffed. When a trump was played to the bare ace, East had a critical return to make. What would you have done?

Many, perhaps most, defenders would do exactly what the original East did. He returned the ◇J. It was not very constructive, since declarer was certain to hold the diamond ace.

South won with the ◇A, drew trumps and played off his winners. The tension was mounting as he reached this end position:

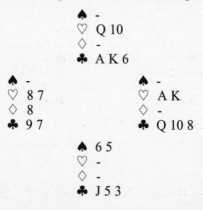

♠ -
♡ Q 10
◇ -
♣ A K 6

West:
♠ -
♡ 8 7
◇ 8
♣ 9 7

East:
♠ -
♡ A K
◇ -
♣ Q 10 8

South:
♠ 6 5
♡ -
◇ -
♣ J 5 3

On the penultimate trump declarer threw a club from dummy. What could East discard? If he threw a top heart, declarer would cross to dummy with a club and ruff the queen of hearts good. East threw a club instead but now declarer cashed the ace and king of clubs, all following, and returned to his hand with a heart ruff to score the established club. The play is known as a trump squeeze.

How could East have prevented the ending? For a trump squeeze to work, declarer needed two good things in dummy: a couple of club entries and two hearts including the queen. It was risky for East to attack the club entries at Trick 3, since South might (and actually did) hold the ♣J. However, it was entirely safe to weaken dummy's heart holding. If East had returned a top heart after winning with the trump ace, no squeeze would have been possible.

Did you spot how declarer can succeed against best defence? East can be end-played with the bare ♠A. After ruffing the heart lead, declarer crosses to the ♣A, ruffs another heart and cashes two top diamonds. He then ruffs a master diamond and ruffs the last heart. A trump to East's bare ace leaves this position:

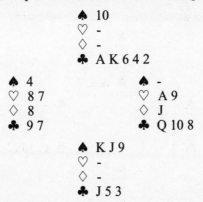

```
              ♠ 10
              ♡ -
              ♢ -
              ♣ A K 6 4 2

    ♠ 4                     ♠ -
    ♡ 8 7                   ♡ A 9
    ♢ 8                     ♢ J
    ♣ 9 7                   ♣ Q 10 8

              ♠ K J 9
              ♡ -
              ♢ -
              ♣ J 5 3
```

A red-suit return will give declarer a ruff-and-discard,

allowing him to dispose of his club loser. The only alternative, a club exit, will be won by South's jack.

Next we will look at a deal or two where the defenders must attack the entries that declarer needs for a squeeze.

Love all
Dealer East

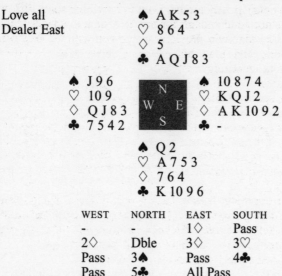

♠ A K 5 3
♡ 8 6 4
◇ 5
♣ A Q J 8 3

♠ J 9 6
♡ 10 9
◇ Q J 8 3
♣ 7 5 4 2

♠ 10 8 7 4
♡ K Q J 2
◇ A K 10 9 2
♣ -

♠ Q 2
♡ A 7 5 3
◇ 7 6 4
♣ K 10 9 6

WEST	NORTH	EAST	SOUTH
-	-	1◇	Pass
2◇	Dble	3◇	3♡
Pass	3♠	Pass	4♣
Pass	5♣	All Pass	

West leads the ◇Q. How will you defend, sitting East?

At the table East overtook and switched to the ♡K. Declarer ducked, to rectify the count, and won the next heart. A diamond ruff was followed by a trump to the ten and a second diamond ruff. This was the position with one trump still to be drawn:

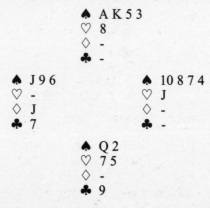

♠ A K 5 3
♡ 8
◇ -
♣ -

♠ J 9 6
♡ -
◇ J
♣ 7

♠ 10 8 7 4
♡ J
◇ -
♣ -

♠ Q 2
♡ 7 5
◇ -
♣ 9

On the last trump declarer threw a heart from dummy and East was squeezed, forced to release his guard in one or other major. How could East have prevented this sad outcome?

If East can foresee the squeeze (not so difficult if he recalls South's heart bid) he may see the need to attack the spade link to dummy. It is not good enough for him to switch to spades when the ♡K is allowed to win. Declarer would win with the ♠Q, ruff two diamonds and play his trumps, again squeezing East in the majors. East must switch to a spade at Trick 2, removing South's ♠Q. If declarer then ducks a heart, to rectify the count, East can win and play a second spade. With no link to the dummy, a squeeze is impossible.

> **TOP TIP**
>
> All squeezes require a two-card threat that contains an entry (for example, A-J opposite a singleton). By playing on the suit that contains the eventual two-card threat, the defenders may be able to kill this essential component of any intended squeeze.

A spade from the ten might cost a trick if declarer has J-9 in the suit but it would not be a critical trick. One heart discard on the spades would not assist declarer. East would still score two tricks with his ♡K-Q-J, enough to put the contract down.

Take the East cards again on the next deal:

East-West game
Dealer South

```
                   ♠ Q 9 3
                   ♡ 9 6 4 3
                   ◇ A J 10
                   ♣ 7 3 2
  ♠ 8 5 2                        ♠ A K J 10 7 6
  ♡ J 10 8 7 5        N          ♡ K Q 2
  ◇ K 8 7 5 3     W     E        ◇ 2
  ♣ -                 S          ♣ 8 6 4
                   ♠ 4
                   ♡ A
                   ◇ Q 9 6 4
                   ♣ A K Q J 10 9 5
```

WEST	NORTH	EAST	SOUTH
-	-	-	1♣
Pass	1♡	1♠	2◇
Pass	3♣	Pass	4NT
Pass	5◇	Pass	6♣
All Pass			

You are unimpressed by South's bidding and think he was very lucky to find such good diamonds in the dummy? We agree with you! Still, sitting East, you will have the chance to see that justice is done. Partner leads the ♠5 (second-best from a bad suit). You win dummy's nine with the ten and must calculate the best return. What is it to be?

At the table East returned an 'easy' king of hearts. Declarer won with the ace, drew trumps and finessed the jack of diamonds successfully. A heart ruff returned the lead to the South hand. Declarer placed East with six spades because West had not raised. Since East had already shown up with three trumps and two hearts, the diamonds could not be 3-3. Declarer saw that he would need to catch West in a trump squeeze. Two more rounds of trumps left these cards out:

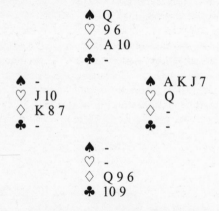

West had no good discard on the penultimate trump. If he threw a diamond declarer would finesse the ◇10, cash the diamond ace and return to his hand with a ruff to score the established ◇Q. If instead West threw a heart, declarer would cross to the ◇10 and ruff a heart good. The ace of diamonds would remain as an entry to the established heart.

No doubt you have seen by now, even if it was not apparent originally, how East might have beaten the squeeze. He needed to switch to his singleton diamond at Trick 2. This would remove one of the entries to dummy before declarer was able to use it (to ruff a heart). No squeeze would result if declarer were simply to run his trump suit. West could retain his length in diamonds, leaving East to guard the heart suit.

How could East calculate that a diamond return was a good idea? Only by foreseeing the squeeze that would otherwise follow. South had bid diamonds and would have no problems if he held K-x-x-x in the suit. (Even if he held K-9-x-x, giving a two-way finesse, he would surely play West for the queen since he was short in the trump suit.)

East therefore needed to break the squeeze that might result, should declarer hold Q-x-x-x in diamonds. He had to attack the entries that would allow declarer to isolate the heart guard in the West hand. Not easy, of course, but in a top-class event like the Bermuda Bowl one would expect most of the East players to find the switch. Or at least to be very annoyed that they had missed it!

The next deal, too, revolves around declarer's communi-

> **TOP TIP**
>
> To prepare for a squeeze, declarer sometimes needs to 'isolate a guard'. In other words, he needs to ruff out one defender's guard in a suit to leave his partner in control of the suit. In defence, you must refuse to assist declarer in this task. Do not thoughtlessly continue to lead your suit, forcing declarer to ruff, if partner's holding may eventually be ruffed out, leaving you liable to a squeeze. Perhaps, instead, you can attack an entry to dummy – one that declarer needs in order to isolate the guard himself.

cations. You can stay in the East seat for the moment.

North-South game
Dealer South

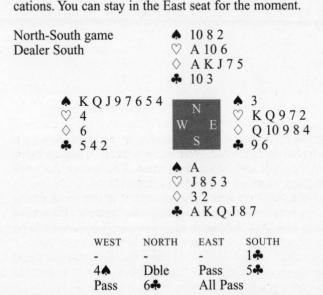

	♠ 10 8 2
	♡ A 10 6
	◇ A K J 7 5
	♣ 10 3

♠ K Q J 9 7 6 5 4	♠ 3
♡ 4	♡ K Q 9 7 2
◇ 6	◇ Q 10 9 8 4
♣ 5 4 2	♣ 9 6

	♠ A
	♡ J 8 5 3
	◇ 3 2
	♣ A K Q J 8 7

WEST	NORTH	EAST	SOUTH
-	-	-	1♣
4♠	Dble	Pass	5♣
Pass	6♣	All Pass	

The deal comes from a teams-of-four match and both tables reached 6♣. At one table West made the rather feeble lead of the ♠K, which could hardly achieve anything. Declarer won and drew two rounds of trumps with the ace and ten. He then ruffed a spade, just in case East had another card in the suit, and drew the last trump. When a heart was played to the ten, East had to surrender one trick with his red-suit return. A simple squeeze yielded yet another trick (after a Vienna Coup of the ♡A) and the contract was made.

At the other table West was more dynamic and reached for a red singleton. A heart lead would have been immediately deadly, as it happens, but West's fingers alighted on the ◇6. Declarer won with dummy's ace and drew trumps in three rounds, noting with interest that West followed three times. He then cashed the ♠A and played a heart to the ten and queen. East was on lead in this position:

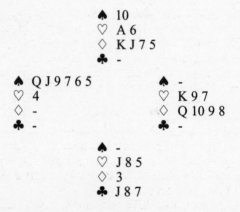

```
              ♠ 10
              ♡ A 6
              ◇ K J 7 5
              ♣ -
♠ Q J 9 7 6 5            ♠ -
♡ 4                     ♡ K 9 7
◇ -                     ◇ Q 10 9 8
♣ -                     ♣ -
              ♠ -
              ♡ J 8 5
              ◇ 3
              ♣ J 8 7
```

Giving the matter insufficient thought, East returned a heart. Declarer won with the jack, crossed to the ♡A and ruffed a spade. His last trump then squeezed East in the red suits.

Look back to the seven-card end position. East does better to return a diamond into dummy's tenace. No squeeze can follow because East can match dummy's lengths in the red suits. For a squeeze to function, declarer needs a one-card threat in his hand and a two-card threat with an entry in the dummy. Since declarer had only one diamond left, facing the king, his one-card threat can only be a heart. It follows that East must attack the entry to the two-card threat by returning a diamond.

A common mistake in defence is to take a winner prematurely, leaving declarer with an entry in the suit. By ducking, you can kill the entry and perhaps also an approaching squeeze. East went wrong on this deal:

Love all
Dealer South

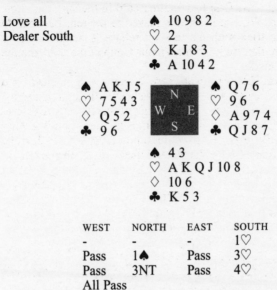

```
                    ♠ 10 9 8 2
                    ♡ 2
                    ◇ K J 8 3
                    ♣ A 10 4 2
  ♠ A K J 5                      ♠ Q 7 6
  ♡ 7 5 4 3            N         ♡ 9 6
  ◇ Q 5 2          W     E       ◇ A 9 7 4
  ♣ 9 6                S         ♣ Q J 8 7
                    ♠ 4 3
                    ♡ A K Q J 10 8
                    ◇ 10 6
                    ♣ K 5 3
```

WEST	NORTH	EAST	SOUTH
-	-	-	1♡
Pass	1♠	Pass	3♡
Pass	3NT	Pass	4♡
All Pass			

South had no reason whatsoever to disturb 3NT — except the familiar one that he wanted to play the hand. West cashed two top spades and had to consider his next move carefully. If he continued with a low spade, for example, the defenders cannot avoid East being squeezed in the minors.

At the table West found the best continuation — a switch to the ♣9. Declarer won with the king and drew trumps in four rounds, throwing a diamond and two clubs from dummy. When he led the ◇10, covered by the queen and king, the second key moment of the deal had been reached. Not sensing any danger, East won with the diamond ace and played back the spade queen, ruffed by declarer. A club to dummy's bare ace left this position:

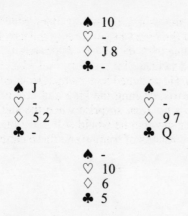

```
              ♠ 10
              ♡ -
              ◇ J 8
              ♣ -
♠ J                      ♠ -
♡ -                      ♡ -
◇ 5 2                    ◇ 9 7
♣ -                      ♣ Q
              ♠ -
              ♡ 10
              ◇ 6
              ♣ 5
```

The ten of spades, which declarer would ruff, squeezed East in the minors and the game was made. Declarer needed a diamond entry to dummy for the squeeze to succeed (the ◇J-8 became his 'two-card threat with an entry'). Had East simply refused to take his ◇A on the first round, the game would have gone down.

To defend well on the next deal, you need a particularly good understanding of squeezes from declarer's point of view.

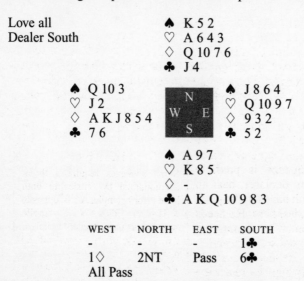

```
Love all            ♠ K 5 2
Dealer South        ♡ A 6 4 3
                    ◇ Q 10 7 6
                    ♣ J 4
♠ Q 10 3         N        ♠ J 8 6 4
♡ J 2        W   E        ♡ Q 10 9 7
◇ A K J 8 5 4    S        ◇ 9 3 2
♣ 7 6                     ♣ 5 2
                    ♠ A 9 7
                    ♡ K 8 5
                    ◇ -
                    ♣ A K Q 10 9 8 3
```

WEST	NORTH	EAST	SOUTH
-	-	-	1♣
1◇	2NT	Pass	6♣
All Pass			

South rebid ambitiously and bought a useful dummy. Even so,

prospects were not especially good. West led the ◇K and declarer rectified the count by discarding a heart. Suppose you were West, with one trick in the bag. What would you do next?

Both major-suit switches looked risky and West did what most players would do. He switched to a trump. Declarer drew trumps and tested the hearts, cashing the king and ace and ruffing the third round. It was no great surprise when the suit divided 2-4. However, declarer saw that he would still make his contract. He played three more rounds of trumps and these cards remained:

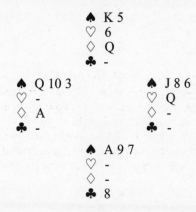

The last trump effected a double squeeze. West had to throw a spade to retain his diamond guard and declarer could afford to release dummy's ◇Q. West had to keep the ♡Q, to guard against dummy's ♡6, so he too had to throw a spade. Declarer then made three spade tricks, scoring the king, ace and nine.

This was an unusual form of double squeeze, where both single threats (♡6 and ◇Q) lay opposite the squeeze card. Such a squeeze is possible only when declarer has an entry to both hands in the pivot suit — spades, here. He needs a spade entry to dummy in case West chooses to abandon diamonds. He needs a spade entry to his hand to reach the potential long spade.

Have you spotted how West

TOP TIP

Some squeezes require a threat accompanied by entries to both hands (for example, A-x-x opposite K-10-x-x). This is a fragile structure. If the defenders switch to the suit, one of the entries will be removed and the squeeze will fail. To diagnose such a switch, you need to visualise declarer's intended squeeze ending.

could spoil declarer's plans? He needs to destroy the double entry in spades by switching to that suit at Trick 2. A switch to the ♠3 would not be good enough. It would exhaust East's guard in the suit (the jack), leaving West exposed to a simple spade-diamond squeeze. West must switch to the ten (or queen) of spades! If you found that defence then — believe us — you have an exceptional understanding of squeeze play.

We will end the chapter, and the book (yes, all good things come to an end), with a deal where declarer achieved a successful strip squeeze. Once again West missed a very difficult chance to defeat the contract. Would you have found it?

Love all
Dealer South

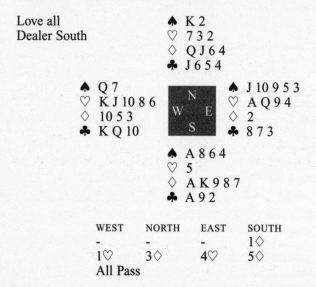

	♠ K 2	
	♡ 7 3 2	
	◇ Q J 6 4	
	♣ J 6 5 4	

♠ Q 7		♠ J 10 9 5 3
♡ K J 10 8 6		♡ A Q 9 4
◇ 10 5 3		◇ 2
♣ K Q 10		♣ 8 7 3

	♠ A 8 6 4	
	♡ 5	
	◇ A K 9 8 7	
	♣ A 9 2	

WEST	NORTH	EAST	SOUTH
-	-	-	1◇
1♡	3◇	4♡	5◇
All Pass			

The deal comes from an end-of-year New York regional and declarer was the USA's Joel Woolbridge. West led the ♡J to East's ace and Woolbridge ruffed the ♡4 return (a club return would have made more sense). Since East was marked with the ace and queen of hearts, it was likely that West held both the missing club honours. However, it was by no means clear how he could be stripped down to three cards in clubs, ready for an end-play.

Woolbridge played the king and ace of spades and ruffed a spade, West discarding a heart. A trump to the ace left this position:

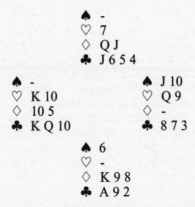

When declarer led his last spade West threw the ♡10. Declarer ruffed with the jack, cashed the bare queen of trumps and returned to hand with a heart ruff to draw the last trump. The desired three-card end position had been achieved. West was down to ♣K-Q-10 and was powerless when declarer led the ♣2. Game made!

Do you see how West can do better? Look back to that seven-card end position. West needed to ruff declarer's losing spade! It may seem a crazy thing to do but the ♡10 was a more precious card than a trump. Declarer would overruff in dummy, cash the ◇Q and ruff a heart to his hand. These cards would be left:

No good for declarer, is it? If he leads a club towards dummy at this stage, West will have a safe exit in hearts. If instead he plays the last trump, West will discard a club and score two of the last three tricks. That's one to remember!